HEALING
THE HEALER INSIDE YOU

HEIDI MORRISON TEACHINGS

Copyright © 2021 Heidi Maria Morrison

All Rights Reserved

No part of this book may be used, reproduced, or utilized in any form or by any means, electronically, or mechanically, including photocopying, recording, or by any information storage and retrieval system without writing permission from the Author Heidi M. Morrison in any manner.

This book is intended as an informational guide. The approaches, and techniques described herein are meant to supplement, and not to be a substitute for professional medical care or treatment. They should not be used to treat a serious ailment without prior consultation with a qualified health care professional.

Morrison, Heidi Maria, – Author
Healing The Healer Inside You - Book Title

Book Cover design by Heidi M. Morrison
Book Covers Photography taken by Sasha Morrison

Book Editing, formatting and images used in book have been provided by Paramount Publishers and are available at Shutterstock for commercial use.

For more information about courses, training, book an appointment and/or contact Heidi M. Morrison visit www.HeidiMorrison.com or email at info@heidimorrison.com

Heidi Morrison Teachings LLC

ISBN: 978-1-80128-201-7

Redondo Beach CA-90277
USA.
www.HeidiMorrison.com

Dedication

With all my love and gratitude, I dedicate this book to our Creator, to that part of God that lives inside You, Me, and All living beings on this planet and in the entire Universe.

Acknowledgment

A special acknowledgment to my Dad, for giving me the best gift. He taught me to always *"listen to my heart"* and find my own answers.

To my daughter, for being so supportive every time.

To all my physical and non-spiritual masters and teachers; for all their wisdom, healing, and guidance.

To my Publication team, thank you for all your efforts in making this book a reality.

To everyone who has helped me put my knowledge and wisdom in this book and made my dream a reality.

About the Author

Heidi M. Morrison is the creator and founder of Heidi Morrison Teachings with *"Healing the Healer Inside You."* She grew up in a musical family and played piano in concerts from the age of 5 until 15.

At the age of 15, Heidi entered the fitness industry. She was teaching a variety of aerobic classes, participated in group aerobic competitions and became a Sports Medicine trainer. Heidi was always about looking for more efficient ways to help herself and her clients. Therefore, she continued to learn and went on to become a Corrective Exercise Specialist, Medical Exercise Specialist, and Massage Therapist. Heidi then began to learn about the Mind and its connection with the sub-conscience, using different types of meditation techniques and Spiritual Healing Modalities.

Heidi M. Morrison is a formally trained Akashic Records Practitioner, Reiki Master, Medium, Breath-work Teacher and Facilitator, Biofield Tuning Practitioner, and a Clairvoyant Reader, Healer, and Teacher. As a former Energy worker, Heidi can teach complex topics in layman's terms.

Today, Heidi has collected an epitome of knowledge; acquired through life-long education, life lessons, and experiences.

Heidi M. Morrison facilitates the Healing process at the cellular level – Activating, Reprograming, Aligning, and Integrating all energetic bodies. With decades of experience under her belt, she aims to teach and guide people so that they can achieve all their aspirations.

> *"The purpose of my life is to share my wisdom and knowledge and to assist others in their journey of realizing their sole purpose."*
>
> −Heidi M. Morrison.

Preface

"Healing the Healer Inside You" puts forward the questions often ignored by society. Many of us believe that the physical realm we live in is all that there is. They are completely unaware of the beauty and marvel of the universe.

This book aims to guide you in understanding the workings of our **mind, body, soul** and how everything is interconnected and interrelated by a web of energy and information within the Universe. It's here to help people transition from the Era of Pisces to the *Era of Aquarius, the Era of Transformation and Spiritual Awakening.*

"Healing the Healer Inside You" combines the teachings of **Science, Physics, and Metaphysics** in a potent, effective, and efficient integrated educational healing material – that provides guidance and practical tools on how energy works, balance Karma, deprogram - reprogram ourselves, return to our Divine Blueprint, serve our Life-Soul purpose, and reach Spiritual Freedom through the process of Ascension and ultimately become *ONE* with our Creator.

Contents

Dedication i
Acknowledgment ii
About the Author.. iii
Preface vi
Chapter 1: Introduction 1

Chapter 2: Awareness 16
   Awareness Changes Everything Around You! 18
   The Science Behind Words 20
   The "Fourth Phase of Water" 23
   The Principle of Vibration 25
   The Principle of Rhythm 26
   The Principle of Causation 27

Chapter 3: The Law of ONE 28
   Yin/Yang Polarities 28
   Balancing the Two Poles 31
   Principle of Polarity 34
   Alchemy 35
   The Principle of Correspondence 38

Chapter 4: The Self 40
   Recapturing Your Self 40
   Self-Love 43

Chapter 5: Karma 50
   The Law of Karma 53
   Forgiveness 55
   Becoming Non-Attach 56
   Taking Responsibility 57
   Free Will 58
   Goodwill 58

Chapter 6: Breathing 59
Modalities of Breathing 60
Moving into the Present Moment 66

Chapter 7: Energetic Anatomy 71
Energetic Anatomy 72
The Chakra System 73
1. Base Chakra (Sanskrit Name: Muladhara) 76
2. Sacral Chakra (Sanskrit name: Svādhisthāna) 82
3. Solar Plexus Chakra (Sanskrit name: Manipura) 87
4. Heart Chakra (Sanskrit name: Anahata) 92
5. Throat Chakra (Sanskrit name: Vissudha) 96
6. Third-Eye Chakra (Sanskrit name: Ajna) 102
7. Crown Chakra (Sanskrit name: Sahasrara) 107

Chapter 8: Consciousness 113
The "I AM" Presence 113
The Three-Fold Flame 114
Ascension 116
Christ Consciousness 118
The Soul Star - 8th Chakra 121
The Seat of the Soul – 9th Chakra 123

Chapter 9: Forgiveness 126
The Ego 128

Chapter 10: Judgment 135
The Principle of Correspondence 136
Learning to Discern 141

Chapter 11: Intentions 144
"The Power of Thought" 145
The Law of Intention 146
Integrity 146
The Principle of Mentalism 148

Chapter 12: Let go 150
    Going with The Flow 152
    Learning to be Flexible 156
    Detaching from The Outcome 157

Chapter 13: Desire 160
    What Do I Want? 160
    Embracing Process 164

Chapter 14: Akashic Records 165
    The Etheric Plane 166
    Accessing the Akashic Records 167
    The Masters and Spiritual Teachers 168

Chapter 15: Wisdom 171
    Difference between Wisdom and Knowledge 173
    Differentiating Truth 175
    Intuition 176

Conclusion 177

Page Left Blank Intentionally

Chapter 1: Introduction

"Many believe the butterfly is associated with the soul. A fitting expression as we embark on this Soulful New Path. A Journey of Shifts, Turns, and Challenges that allow us to morph into more evolved Beings."

–Ann Mortifee.

The **New Era of Transformation**, or the year with higher frequencies of light, began its transition in January 2020. This was when the world entered the **'Aquarian Era of Spiritual Awakening.'** It is believed that this year marked the return of the divine feminine energy. This was much needed to rebalance the scale between masculine and feminine, which had tipped in the Piscean Era.

January 2020 was believed to be the month when Pluto and Saturn got aligned and hence marked the advent of the most potent cosmic energies to emerge. This alignment is an indication for the **Birth of Mother Earth** and **humanity to Ascend** to higher levels of Consciousness. This provides every human with a chance to shift their attention from materialism to spirituality, making humans reflect on what is important in life and the purpose of their soul incarnated on this planet.

"We are all part of a greater whole, connected and interrelated by a web of energy and information."

–Heidi M. Morrison.

In the light of Covid-19, there seems to be a strong connection between the Ascension of the planet and the transition into the New Era. This was mainly made possible due to the learning opportunity that this pandemic has provided us. There seems to be some spiritual synchrony, and the lesson that it intends to teach us has been unprecedented. Covid-19 is a learning episode for all of us to evaluate our lives from a completely different perspective as we liberate ourselves from all the sufferings we have accumulated over our lifetimes. We need to lessen the burden on our chest and wake up to this new era and give our life a fresh start. Gone are the days when we used to live life in complacency and ignorance. We need to realize where we belong and return home to become *"One"* again and to *"stop the Wheel of Karma."* We need to implement ***"The Law of Divine Love and Oneness"*** in our lives. This law continually reminds us that we are inevitably connected to one source, and all our actions inadvertently affect the collective consciousness and unconsciousness of the entire universe. We cannot see our actions, behaviors, and attitudes in isolation, which is why the act of giving and making someone's life better is so fulfilling and rewarding.

"Feel the love of God; then in every person, you will see the face of the Father, the light of love, which is in all. You will find a magic, living relationship uniting the trees, the sky, the stars, all people, and all living things, and you will feel oneness with them. This is the code of divine love."

-Paramahansa Yogananda.

Purpose and Inspiration to Write This Book

My journey of self-liberation and self-realization has been my inspiration to write this book. In these challenging times, if humanity doesn't unite, we are bound to undergo irreversible damage. Covid-19 has gotten us all to revisit our spiritual values and how things can be done differently. I've always had this burning desire to give back to humanity in some way or the other. This global pandemic seems to be an incredible opportunity to do so. Every coin has two sides, and through this book, I intend to enlighten people with the positive aspect of the disease-stricken world. There is no denying the fact that things have deteriorated at an unprecedented rate, and if something is not working out, there must be a better and different way.

Hence, I consider my responsibility to introduce people to viable and sustainable ways to cope with this pandemic. Maybe the rules of righteous living had been set a long time ago, but we have been ignorant human beings – forgetting our purpose here, on our home, Planet Earth. Maybe this is a time to reminisce all that we have taken for granted and how we can change our approach from reactive to proactive. We need to alter the lens through which we see the world, apply our logical reasoning, and adopt all those measures that will equip us to better fight this condition.

"The world we have created is a product of our thinking; it cannot be changed without changing our thinking. If we want to change the world, we have to change our thinking. No problem can be

solved from the same consciousness that created it. We must learn to see the world anew."

-Albert Einstein.

During my spiritual quest, I realized that the power to create and bring about change is an attribute that lives within us. We just need to reach out and leverage it, put it to use, and implement it as an agent of change. We cannot turn a blind eye to all that is happening around us and live an ignorant life. We need to take back control and see how we can save ourselves, humanity, and our planet from our ignorant, ill-informed, and impulsive decisions. We need to tap into our spiritual and emotional energy reserves and focus on creating *'Good Karma.'* We cannot play with our destinies and then later blame external factors for making our life miserable. We need to understand that the reigns of our lives are in our hands, and nothing can motivate us to do better than ourselves.

I was continuously questioning myself; What is the reason for my existence? What is the purpose for which I have been incarnated at this time and space? Is there anything that I can do to better my own life and the life of others?

That is when I decided to focus on comprehending my spiritual self and gain a deep understanding of what lies within me. Developing and nurturing spirituality is as fundamental as eating a well-balanced diet, maintaining a physical routine, and building meaningful relationships.

I was in need and in a never-ending quest to know the truth. I wanted to spiritually awaken myself and others; to bring my faith back to life. I placed my trust in my Spiritual Guides, my Angels, who guided me explore and learn the different healing modalities. Teachers appeared in my life as if they were magic. The synchronicities of events were inexplicable. I knew deep inside myself that I was at the right place, at the right time, learning from the right teacher. It was fascinating, as I never knew what I was meant to learn. I just felt it inside of myself, and nothing could stop me; - my soul craved this intensely.

The joy I felt when I drove to meet my teachers was inexplicable. All I can say, ***"My Soul was (and is!) super happy!"*** I was determined to unleash my true potential and reservoir of happiness that had somehow deterred me from being myself. I was yearning to find and feel true happiness from within myself.

When I set out to seek **'Higher Knowledge'** in the form of spiritual freedom, I realized how great and infinite the power of knowledge is. If once you reach out to your internal energies and embark on the self-fulfilling journey of attaining knowledge, there is no going back. From that point onwards, your life is bound to change for the better. If, for whatever reason, you abandon your spiritual journey abruptly, you will only create havoc and confusion within yourself and not be able to take control of the elements that determine the trajectory of your life.

Once you engage with your spiritual energies and gain knowledge and apply it to your life to feel its full impact, you will have to do it with full passion and vigor. You cannot venture out into this domain half-heartedly or without proper direction. Spiritual practice can be aptly called as an act of ongoing devotion that never stops. It serves as a means to surrender yourself to life and to trust the natural order of things to unravel themselves in due time. This will allow you to explore the wonders and mysteries of life hidden within you.

I want to share with you some of the different healing modalities I learned, practiced, and now teach. These different healing modalities allowed me to get to know myself deep into my soul, raising my level of awareness and expanding me into varying levels of consciousness.

What are Healing Modalities?

These are energy spiritual healing procedures that restore and balance the flow of energy throughout the mind, body, and soul. They are directly connected to your well-being as they focus on your emotional, spiritual, and physical aspects. Let me introduce you to some different kinds of healing modalities that have helped me heal from the inside and help me reach the place where I am today.

Reiki

A spiritually guided life force energy. Mikao Usui, a Japanese Buddhist developed it in 1922. The word itself splits into two, *'Rei'* means *God's Wisdom* or *Higher Power,* and *'Ki'* means *Universal life-force energy.* It is administered by either direct contact by the hands, or by hands hovering right above your body.

A Reiki session is an ethereal sensation which radiates and pulses throughout your body, and around you. Reiki treats the person physically, emotionally, and spiritually. Reiki is a natural and harmless modality of spiritual healing and self-improvement which can be utilized by everyone irrespective of their age. It can work side-by-side with other therapeutic or medical techniques to relieve side-effects and promote recovery.

We all deal with stressful situations daily. It can drain the body and cause fatigue. Reiki has the power to remove stress from the mind and tension from the body. Reiki also has the qualities and gentleness to transition people into the afterlife peacefully. Not only can it help those who are close to depart from this earth, but the alternative healing practice can assist those grieving a loved one as well. Reiki is not limited just to human beings; you can use the power of Reiki to heal animals, plants, bless your food, water, and even physical spaces.

Breathwork

A prevailing approach to healing and self-exploration that amalgamates the teachings from anthropology, modern conscious research, various fields of psychology, Eastern spiritual practices and mystical traditions found around the world. Breathwork is a potent modality that will help you move toward wholeness. A breathwork session combines accelerated breathing with evocative music in a particular setting to illicit the most emotions. With the person keeping their eyes closed while they lay on a mat, the person uses their own breath and the music in the room to enter a non-ordinary state of consciousness. This state of consciousness activates the individual's psyche's natural inner healing intelligence, bringing them into a particular set of internal experiences.

"By working on forming a complete and harmonious undivided whole-self, we begin raising above the limited boundaries of our body ego and begin to regain our full individuality."

-Heidi M. Morrison.

By utilizing our innate inner wisdom, we can use this as an opportunity to work toward our physical, mental, emotional, and spiritual bodies, promoting healing and developmental change.

Akashic Records

A Sanskrit word that refers to a *'body of mystical knowledge.'* The Akashic Records hold the infinite records of every soul that has ever been created – from the time the soul first arose from the Source until it returns home. It does not matter how "new" or "old" a soul is, the Akashic records hold the entirety of an individual's feelings, thoughts, actions and deeds from each and every lifetime.

Some people visualize the energy of the Akasha as an infinite library, with each "book" representing a lifetime. Others look at the Akashic Record as a computer that has all the information stored on its hard disk. The truth of the matter is, the Akashic field is an integral part and is connected to the All. You possess your own Akashic Record Keepers, Teachers, Masters and Beings of Light that keep track of all your information. You can access these spiritual guides and they will answer any and all questions that you may have about your current life, or your past lives which may be affecting you to this day.

When you come to terms with the fact that you came into existence with a plan, it is beneficial for you to access that plan's information. We incarnate to complete Karma, fulfill our past life vows, be with someone special, and support people who are part of our soul family and circle. The human challenge is that as soon as we're born, this plan is erased from our memories. At times in our lives, we feel blocked, constricted, or disappointed because we don't remember why we chose our families or situations. We may feel life is unfair or challenging.

I access the Akashic Records to help you understand and learn from information about these situations as well as, to heal and end emotional pain accumulated in your body and mind. You can ask questions about health, career, relationships, life purpose, self-esteem, and abundance. [1]

---

[1] More information about Akashic Records or book a session with me at www.heidimorrison.com

Biofield Tuning

It is established on the principle of vibration; everything in the universe resonates with its own frequency – its own vibration. *Sound Healing* is possible because our human bodies are not solid. Our bodies are rhythmic and harmonic. Contracting a disease can indicate that we have gone out of tune or the body's vibrational rate has lost its rhythm. Biofield tuning can bring "sync" us back to our body's natural rhythmic pattern, help assist the immune system, and help stimulate the body to heal itself. Because our bodies are made up of water, and water conducts sound, the body is an excellent resonator for sound. These vibratory sounds travel through the body, and help remove energetic blockages, thereby relieving stagnation, pain and increasing the flow of Chi. Biofield tuning enables the body to find balance and homeostasis.

Homeostasis is fundamental to healing the physical, mental, and emotional bodies as it activates the healing, deep into a cellular level. Biofield tuning is rich in resonance and vibration, connecting and supporting the body's natural frequencies.

The sound waves produced by the forks vibrate and travel deep within the body along our energy pathways, affecting human physiology and accessing our sense of space, memory, and healing. It stimulates and balances the body's physical energy field to promote healing and inner harmony, helping us to integrate body, mind, and soul.

They are many ways I use Biofield tuning for myself and my clients. Some of these methods include; Tuning the Biofield,

Adrenal glands reset, Brain waves balance, Meridian flush, Harmonize Relationships, Releasing stress, anxiety, and much more.[2]

Meditation

They are many types of meditation; mindful, spiritual, movement, mantra, transcendental, visualization, sound, and so on. We can meditate sitting, lying down, or even while standing. There is no good or bad way to meditate.

Meditation has the power to relax brainwave patterns. Through meditation, the mind can enter a state of deep rest, allowing the physical body to relax as well. Through regular practice of meditation, you can overcome mental, emotional, physical, and spiritual challenges in your life – where anxiety decreases, and emotional stability increases.

All the different healing modalities can help you spiritually by connecting you with your inner self, which can provide you with guidance and clarity when facing adversities and making decisions in life.

Let's suppose you suffer from chronic pain, dealing with negative life force energy, emotions such as anger, fear, jealousy, guilt, insecurity, resentment, stress, or others. In that case, these healing modalities can help alleviate those heavy burdens from your mind, body, and spirit.

---

[2] More information about Biofield Tuning or book a session with me at www.heidimorrison.com

It is still alive in my memory an experience; that was communicated to me loud and clear while I was in a trance at a breath-work healing session in New Mexico:

"...We are here to help you, and you help heal others..."

At that moment, my entire being was filled with an inexplicable sense of energy. I have always been in service for helping others, but this was much bigger than that. It was communicated telepathically to pass on my spiritual knowledge to others. Even though I did not have the entire action, I felt I had to work my way around it. You wouldn't believe it, but the moment I decided to take my destiny into my own hands, I started receiving dreams – one after the other. I felt honored and blessed to gain spiritual direction from my spiritual guides. I was filled with an inexplicable but divine feeling of contentment from within. I had no doubts about its genuine-ty, as it started to dominate my entire existence.

One morning, I woke up repeating the **"Healing the Healer Inside You"** phrase. It felt as if it was imprinted on my mind so firmly, I could see through the fact that I needed to heal myself inside out thoroughly to transfer all the healing power and knowledge into others. As I set out on the quest to gain spiritual freedom, the journey required me to muster a lot of energy from within myself and was rather painful. It was like being thrown in the middle of the ocean amongst deadly sharks that could attack me at any moment. The struggle to keep swimming and not become the shark's prey was real. There seemed to be no escape from this situation, and the shore was far away from sight as well. The only hope was to trust in God and keep swimming until things were restored to normal.

That was the time when I surrounded myself with nothing except meditation, prayer, and spiritual developmental healing classes. I did my best to work on my innate capabilities and always keep up my spirit. I knew one thing for sure; the fieriest energies come from inside of me, and it was up to me how I channeled them in the right direction to reconnect and find my true self. I was doing all that was in my discretion to get back on my feet, and I wasn't going to let anyone pull me down. When I finally made my way to the shore and achieved a sense of stability in my life, I left no stone unturned in making sure that core values were in sync with my spiritual knowledge. I did the maximum that I could, to keep myself afloat and work on my mental de-programming, reprogramming and spiritual development. My spiritual guides began to bless me with enlightening dreams in the form of various words, pictures, and phrases. I started receiving telepathic messages that filled me with a sense of irreversible confidence.

My lifelong desire to teach and help heal others has finally come to fruition as I get this opportunity to compile my book based on my spiritual experiences and learnings. Teaching is my passion, and it gives me a sense of purpose and direction in life. I could never have imagined a life where I wouldn't have been able to pass on my life learnings and only contain it within myself. The only way I could see myself climbing out of the dungeons of self-doubt, low self-esteem, and despair, was to channel my energies towards something productive.

Throughout the years, I have learned, practiced, and taught many different healing modalities. Today, I integrate the knowledge that has been given to me from physical and non-physical spiritual masters and teachers. *"Healing the Healer Inside You"* combines the teachings of *Science, Physics, and Metaphysics*. It is a potent, effective, and efficient integrated healing modality that you can learn.

Through my teachings, I aim to enlighten you with some fundamentals that I believe everyone must integrate into their daily lives. You will learn *how the* **Universe works,** *the basics of* **Energy,** **Energetic Anatomy,** **Akashic Records,** **Karma,** **Deprograming, Reprogramming, Spiritual Freedom,** *and much more.*

Lessons You Can Learn from This Book

The life lessons that I have learned are too vast to be encapsulated in a single book. I will try my best to leverage the spiritual tools and guides – so you can find your purpose in life.

Peace, Love, and Joy are all found within you, and the entire universe seems to work in your favor if you have aligned these energies within yourself.

Life requires us to follow some core ground rules, such as having Integrity, and for us to follow Universal Spiritual Laws and Principles in order to achieve a Happier, Joyful and Abundant Life.

Consciously or unconsciously, we all are co-creators. Unfortunately, many of us have forgotten the real purpose of our existence. It is essential to do some soul-searching to emerge stronger and wiser.

It is important to re-evaluate our priorities and start living our own lives and create what we actually want. This can only happen once we pay attention to our own internal self, and work toward our own self-healing.

"Knowing yourself is the beginning of all wisdom."

-Aristotle.

You are the most important person in your life, and you need to nurture yourself. Honor every part of you – your body, your mind, and your soul. Learn to say; *"Thank you"* and *"I Love you"* to every part of your being. Take yourself out for a date, meditate, spend some time in a serene place that soothes your senses, exercise, and eat healthy. When something goes wrong, remember to practice empathy, compassion, and acceptance. Go on a digital detox and take a vacation without taking any electronic gadget with you. The liberating feeling that you will feel will make you realize that you are enough for yourself, and nothing matters in life when you are peaceful and content at heart.

You need to take care of yourself as no one else is going to come and do it for you, because the happier you are, the more positive energy you will attract as a consequence. Happiness is contagious, and you can inspire others to be happy, by being happy with yourself. Renew your membership with yourself – and guess what, it's completely free of cost!

Chapter 2: Awareness

"Today is a unique and special day. It is unlike any other day you have ever experienced. If you assume that today is like every other day, you will never notice today's uniqueness. If you practice keen awareness, you will get to savor today's uniquely wonderful qualities."

–Jonathan Lockwood Huie.

If you were to concentrate your energies on something meaningful consciously, you would realize what is truly worth your energy and attention, and what is not.

Have you ever been through that phase where your issues and worries tend to vanish as you shift your focus to things that truly matter?

The entire universe is made up of energy and information; it is all around and inside you; – the only difference is that it takes different forms and shapes.

Have you ever wondered how much energy you are utilizing productively, and how much energy you are wasting that diverts you from the more essential agendas in your life?

Have you ever thought to yourself;

- *What motivates me?*
- *What is the driving force that propels you to work hard towards a specific goal in life?*

- *Are they materialistic things or some form of emotional and mental energies that bind you to your target?*

In the universe that we live in, we are invariably governed by transformative and unalterable laws. A major one being the *"Law of Attraction"* – the concept of *'Like attracting Like.'*

You possess energy equivalent to a giant *'Magnet.'* This means that you are made to attract energy. Whichever state you are in, it is the result of your subconscious wiring your mind and your constant reinforcement by dwelling on it. Remember that you and your life, are a product of what you let your brain consume and the emotions you ruminate upon.

The flow of energy that we are talking about foremost manifests itself in the form of *'Awareness.'* As soon as you decide to open the doors of your heart, you are preparing yourself to begin your journey of spiritual growth and freedom.

Your heart has the power to drive you into a multi-dimensional space. It fills you with extraordinary energy, which ultimately allows you to synchronize and get in line with a higher vibrational experience. When you open your heart, you don't just become accessible to your true self (your Soul), but also to an array of Angelic, Celestial Beings ready to assist you with their unconditional love, compassion, wisdom, and guidance. However, more than often, even if you are flexible enough to have an open heart, the ultimate control lies in your mind. If you try to make your heart receptive by attempting to control it through your mind, you will keep struggling to come to terms with it. It can become quite overwhelming and energy-consuming as your mind becomes the focal point of all your energies rather than your heart.

What you need to practice, is the ability to trust your heart with the experiences that will follow. Resonate with what your heart is trying to tell you, and let the light in your heart shine through, see for yourself what you are capable of. Let the flow of energy fill your heart and open it up to unique experiences.

A great way to focus your attention and to move into the present moment, is by creating awareness. Educate yourself by reading on empowering content that shines through your spirit, take a self-development class, learn a healing modality, practice meditation, or other healing modalities that will help you heal and get to know yourself better. Get your energy to flow towards things that you genuinely want to create. Do not let unimportant, distracted, or non-beneficial thoughts bring you down.

"To invest in improving and getting to know yourself better. It is the best investment you could ever make and one which you can harvest over lifetimes."

–Heidi M. Morrison.

Awareness Changes Everything Around You!

When you are aware of your own emotions and feelings, you are better able to project them towards others. Hence, to reach a higher level of awareness, you will need to expand your consciousness. *Begin by concentrating on your breathing and all things around you.*

Consciousness is an individual state of awareness about their external environment, internal thoughts, feelings, and actions. One must be awake and aware to experience consciousness.

Each of us carries an irrevocable amount of energy to bring about a change. However, many of us tend to settle in and follow the herd. To reach any level of consciousness, it is essential for you to primarily focus your awareness on your own Self; learn to reflect and comprehend who you truly are, at a deeper, more intrinsic level – at the *level of your Soul.*

Introspection provides us with the unique opportunity to look beyond what meets the physical eye and not take things for face value alone. External influences and personal internalized biases affect everyone, but when our level of self-awareness is high, we are more confident in what we express, think, feel, act, and even how we react.

Self-mastery has a unique sense of accomplishment associated with it. Attaining the level of true self-awareness in itself is self-mastery. It means that you are true to yourself through a deep holistic understanding of both, your internal and external self. As a consequence, this will make you indulge in self-love and know - deep inside you, that you do not need to prove yourself to anyone whatever you do. However, this is only ever possible when you are at peace with yourself.

It is also essential to know that self-esteem, self-worth, and self-love, are all connected by self-acceptance and closely linked to each other, as the relationship between each one of them will determine the love you extend to yourself. For this reason, it is important to prioritize yourself and engage in activities that strengthen your personality's self-love component.

Being self-aware is a fundamental component when it comes to the expansion of self-esteem and self-love. In order to live a happy and content life, you need to know what to absorb into your system and what to filter out.

Self-love is something that takes birth inside you, and as it grows, you will realize that it will expand outward – spreading positive vibrations all around your personality and the external world. This means that you will fully accept yourself, treat yourself with respect and kindness, as you nurture and foster your growth and wellbeing.

Self-love encompasses how you treat yourself physically, mentally, and emotionally through the countless thoughts, actions, and feelings you have about yourself. When your awareness increases, you will be able to learn about yourself on a more profound level. You will be able to control your thoughts, feelings, and actions, which as a consequence, will resonate with positive people, and ultimately the world around you.

"Your visions will become clear only when you can look into your own heart. Who looks outside, dreams, who looks inside awakes."

-Carl Jung.

The Science Behind Words

When we translate our thoughts and feelings into words, it has a significant impact on how we behave and lead our lives living forward. Every time we speak, we create a *road*. The quality of that road and how far it goes is directly related to the *Integrity* of our words.

The dictionary defines integrity as –

"Integrity is the practice of being honest and showing a consistent and determined constancy to strong moral and ethical principles and values."

Oxford Dictionary.

In ethics, integrity is considered as the honesty and truthfulness of one's actions. To have integrity means to have principles and to abide by those set principles consistently – throughout all the various parts of the self.

Words carry lots of energy that affects us, every living being on this planet and therefore the entire Universe. If we tap into the power of words (the fact that voice is made of vibrations), we can use that energy to get together or apart, create or destroy.

Several studies and experiments have been done in this regard, where plants were placed in three different rooms and subjected to three different kinds of treatments. The first one was showered with kind words, the other was subjected to rude words, and the last one was kept in silence. After the experiment, all three plants' growth was noted, and it turned out that the one exposed to gentle and kind words grew more than the other two. What does this tell us about the power and effect of words?

Every time we say something, we just don't utter mere words in the form of a sentence. We actually create an ever-lasting impact on the mind of the receiver, as well as in our own mind. Words possess this magical ability to refresh your mood, relieve you of mental noise by providing perspective, and fill you with energy and good vibrations.

"Words are powerful and magical forces of creation. As we speak, they create our reality. Be aware of your words today."

-Heidi M. Morrison.

It is recommended for us to surround ourselves in the company of good, positive people, because they think and speaks positively, which inevitably will affect our thought processes, in addition to our emotional and even physical state. When you utter positive, uplifting words, the world around you, starts to appear more welcoming as you attract more positive energy into your life.

Water

Water is defined as a colorless, odorless, and transparent liquid that forms the seas, lakes, rivers, and rain and is the base structure of the fluids within living organisms. Water is fundamental for all life; without it, every living organism would die. Every single cell in our body requires water to function correctly. Animals, plants, the ground, the air, all consist of water molecules, and they are all dependent on water for their existence.

The "Fourth Phase of Water"

In this famous book, *"The Fourth Phase of Water: Beyond Solid, Liquid, and Vapor,"* Gerald H. Pollack takes his readers on the fascinating journey of exploring the fourth phase of water. This phase has some hidden truths and meanings, unique enough to stir the most still minds and evoke the curiosity of people who understand the beauty of nature and the **Power of Words.** He lays down how essential it is to understand the basic structure of water and the instrumental influence it presents – more than what meets the eye.

Gerald Pollack was undoubtedly one of the pioneering scientists in the field of water research. He was among those who took up the daunting task of navigating the perils of water by conducting in-depth research to understand water's three-dimensional structure.

Gerald's theory about EZ water, a negatively charged layer created between a positively charged bulk water and a hydrophilic structure. The energy for building these water structures comes from sunlight (infra-red radiation), which is the longest in the spectrum of light. This is also known as the exclusion zone that we call the fourth phase of water.

If we were to see our body's molecular buildup, *99% of our molecules* are water molecules, because they are smaller than other kinds of molecules in our body. The 99% of molecules in our body create a fluid environment for more important molecules of life in our body. The healing power of water can also be attributed to this phenomenon, as the water quality increases by its mineral content and depends on the high EZ content. We all know that water has been giving life to this planet since time immemorial and has been used by several factions in sacred healing rituals and other holy ceremonies.

Water carries specific energetic properties. It can fill your sense of being with serenity, calmness, and composure. It has high purifying qualities that nurture, clean, and sustain everything it comes in contact with. It will fill your life with sustainability and joy once you learn how to draw in on water's energetic essence.

"The entire Universe is kept in place with laws and principles of nature that are capable of controlling our internal energies. When we develop a conscious understanding of these laws, we can recognize and acknowledge them in our surroundings, utilizing them to the best of our abilities."

–Heidi M. Morrison.

The Principle of Vibration

"Nothing rests; everything moves; everything vibrates."

-Hermes Trismegistus.

Under the umbrella of this principle, we believe in the overarching base that **nothing rests** and that everything is in a constant state of motion, and **everything vibrates.** This extends to all forms of life in the form of energy, matter, and spirit that they are simply vibrations in different forms. It's just a change in the manifestation of the difference in the wavelengths and energy frequencies across the electromagnetic spectrum. If we observe these vibrations at the highest rate and intensity, they would almost be invisible and appear motionless like a spinning wheel at rest. Whilst, at the lowest level of vibrations, we observe the same phenomenon as the object seems to be at rest. Between these two ends of the continuum lies a series of manifestations, each with varying rates, intensity and having their own unique phenomena.

The same principle is applicable to the thoughts that occupy our minds, each one having its own frequency and rate of vibration. If we were to control it, it could be done like you tune an instrument to get varying frequencies of results. The level of self and environmental mastery would depend on which vibration level you fine-tune it to. When you make a conscious effort to make sense of the deep, underlying concepts behind frequency, vibration, resonance, and harmony, you will find yourself in a much more empowering space regarding your thoughts, emotions, and feelings.

The Principle of Rhythm

"Everything flows, out and in; everything has its tides; all things rise and fall; the pendulum swing manifests in everything; the measure of the swing to the right is the measure of the swing to the left; Rhythm compensates."

–Hermes Trismegistus.

This principle believes in the nature of things being in continuous evolution. The truth, according to this principle, is that everything that has ever existed, or currently exists, is in measured motion, to and from one point to another, in and out, back and forth, like a pendulum between the opposite poles of the Principle of Polarity. This form of energy may rise, subside, and flow when needed, but will never cease.

When you consciously tune in to the Principle of Rhythm, you consciously embrace the notion that every mental state exists in Rhythm, and you need to learn to polarize yourself to the degree which you desire. When you find yourself in complete awareness of this principle and how it manifests in your life in different forms, you need to ground yourself to keep the pendulum from swinging too much, or out of rhythm by going into extremes.

The Principle of Causation

"Every cause has its effect; every effect has its cause; everything happens according to law. Chance is but a name for law not recognized. There are many planes of causation, but nothing escapes the law."

-*Hermes Trismegistus.*

The idea behind this principle is that there is a cause for every effect and an effect for every cause. This follows that everything happens for a reason, and we are not left on chance. If that was the case, our life would be in the doldrums right now.

If we use this principle to empower ourselves in different walks of life, we will be able to strengthen ourselves by making a conscious choice and rising above our current state of thoughts and transition from being an effect to others to being our own cause. You will start taking things in your hands proactively rather than just reacting to situations.

When a person feels stressed and frazzled, they are often pushed into the reactive zone and cannot handle things level-headedly. You need to consciously become the experiences you desire to live, rather than waiting for life to happen. When you embark on the journey of finding your true self and take control of your personality, character, mood, and environment – you will finally discover and tune yourself with your Higher Self. The key is to develop a strong relationship within yourself and truly know and understand *"what you want."*

Chapter 3: The Law of ONE

The law of One tells us;

"Every single Soul, incarnate and discarnate, is connected at the level of the collective conscious and unconscious within the Higher Self.

We are all part of an extraordinary, energetic living substance called God.

The purpose of this energetic living substance is to create more energy.

When we live in peace, harmony, and unity, we not only increase our level of vibration, but also increase the level of vibration of the entire energetic living substance.

When we live in conflict, disharmony, and disunity, we not only decrease our own level of vibration, but also decrease the level of vibration of the entire energetic substance.

Because we are all connected and part of this ONE energetic living substance, everything we think, say, the way we feel and what we do, affects every Soul."

Yin/Yang Polarities

It is to believe that all humans nurture two forces within themselves: Yin and Yang. They are complete opposites, and yet they must be kept dynamically integrated within each other. Yin refers to feminine energies, while Yang refers to masculine energies. Giving is an action of our masculine energy and receiving is an action of our feminine energy. Both the Yin and Yang elements manifest in varying degrees and proportions in a person's character. You can either choose to unleash the dominant side (masculine) or have a more passive personality (feminine). This is explained by the Taoist Symbol Yin-Yang.

False dichotomies such as soft and hard, right and wrong, light and dark are often described using Yin and Yang. These dichotomies are often labeled as false because nothing is completely good or downright bad. There has to be at least some trace of bad in a good act and something good about a heinous act. This can also be explained through the analogy that even though wood seems hard on its surface, it has soft tissue layers inside it. Hence, the Yin/Yang symbol internalizes the characteristic of the opposite element. Yin and Yang are considered two different parts of the same whole and both must co-exist in mutual harmony, as one cannot exist without the other. They would have no contrast without each other. We would not appreciate the light if we did not know what darkness is and vice versa. This helps us understand how masculinity and femininity are poles apart, and the spiritual energies that lie between them help make sense of them.

Feminine energy can be described as a passive force with nurturing capabilities and understood as *Yin*. On the other hand, *Masculine* energy is represented by *Yang* and is an action-oriented force that is direct and assertive. Both energies, depend on each other for existence. This explains the behavior of some men with a tremendous amount of masculine energy, who tend to gravitate towards women (with greater feminine energy) who are passive, receptive, and possess nurturing qualities. In the presence of such a female, he feels empowered by his masculine traits because the women do not overshadow his masculinity. On the contrary, some women prefer to be with men who have greater masculine energy because they make them feel protected and secure in a dynamic world. The men proactively take charge and do not exhibit the feminine traits of taking the back seat and being passive. Do you realize how the Yin and Yang subtly complement each other, as the masculinity of the man while also defining the femininity of a woman?

We are born with balanced energies, but we often tend to tip the scale and lose the balance that nature has bestowed upon us. The *Yang* element of our personalities begins to show up more when we become aggressive and dominant. Other personalities that are submitted and subservient are ones with the *Yin* element shining through strongly.

Neither of these extremities are beneficial for us because, if we empower either the Yin or Yang to overstep boundaries, the dynamic tension between these two poles will lose its connection. We could find ourselves in a very unbalanced state of mind that can lead to disastrous outcomes. At that point in time, it is crucial to restore this lost balance, and fine-tune with our internal energies to reestablish dynamic tension between the two poles.

Balancing the Two Poles

If we are to establish balance and work towards creating a unified world within ourselves, we need to take inspiration from the Yin and Yang energies. It is important to see them as individual and complementary parts of a balanced and unified whole. The balance of Yin and Yang is like seeing life through a filter. You start to appreciate the subtleties and be more receptive to change. You don't see things in black and white anymore, and always try to find a middle ground between your heart, and your mind. Yin and Yang's energies are all around us in the form of dark and light, the sun and moon, male and female, and so on. Balancing these two complementary energies are key to obtaining the best quality of life.

Masculine or Yang characteristics energies include:

- *Determination*
- *Analytical*
- *Competitive*
- *Rational*
- *Specific*
- *Hard*
- *Action-oriented*

Feminine or Yin characteristics energies include:

- *Calmness and Stillness*

- *Nurturing*
- *Emotional*
- *Soft*
- *Collaborative*
- *Passionate*
- *Intuitive*
- *Creative*

You might be inclined towards either of the two elements, Yin or Yang. You might feel like the more dominant counterpart, and that the action-oriented side of you takes over you at certain times. Whereas there will be times when all you would like to do is read a book, meditate, or just take a nap and relax.

Balancing these two energies is very important because, it determines your interaction with yourself, and the external world. It is essential to acknowledge and embrace your divine feminine core energy, as well as your divine masculine core energy, as both are equally important in shaping *"You," "Become One."*

Practice

Take a moment to honor yourself and evaluate your life.

Identify and recognize whether you need more feminine energy or masculine energy to balance your own self.

o **To increase your feminine energy,**

Focus on your creativity, intuition, and passion. This can be done by invoking peace and calmness into yourself.

You can do this by lighting candles, playing soft music, and creating a sacred space of relaxation and calmness.

Practicing breathing exercises, meditation, painting, singing, writing, and giving yourself time for introspection will also help further these energies.

Once you have achieved that calm space, ask yourself:

- *What makes me happy?*
- *What am I grateful for?*
- *What motivates me?*
- *How do I feel?*

o *To increase your masculine energy,*

Focus your attention on putting your ideas and vision into perspective and then into actions.

When concentrating on your masculine energy, ask yourself:

- *Which ideas are beneficial for me to put into action?*
- *Which strategy and plan are beneficial for me to follow?*
- *Will it be beneficial for me to receive support from others? If yes, then what are those sources?*

It is crucial to balance your Yin and Yang energies flowing inside you and to align them with **'Integrity'** and **'Morals'** within yourself.

"By creating a healthy relationship between our own self, and balancing our Yin and Yang energies, we'll find harmony and fulfillment within."

–Heidi M. Morrison.

Principle of Polarity

"Everything is dual; everything has poles; everything has its pair of opposites; like and unlike are the same; Opposites are identical in nature, but different in degree; extremes meet; all truths are but half-truths; all paradoxes may be reconciled."

–*Hermes Trismegistus.*

This encompasses one of the most instrumental Hermetic Formulas based upon true scientific principles. Upon further study, we realize that this principle intends to tell us that everything has two poles and two opposite aspects with varying degrees existing between the ends of the continuum.

The Principle of Polarity states that many things that may appear as total opposites on the face of it, might just be varying degrees of the same thing, such as the North and the South Pole, East and West, Hot and Cold, Night and Day or the two poles of the same thing.

When we have the vision to see these polarities in the real world, we can get rid of the opposing energies rising within us by being in a neutral state and observing things. We can completely turn over the situation and transform our thoughts by raising our vibration from the polarized state and making peace with the neutral state.

To better understand this, it helps if we look at everyday examples. If we try to understand the phenomenon of hot and cold, we will realize that cold is the absence of heat, and when heat finishes, the cold begins. There is no concept of absolute heat or absolute cold. The different states of hotness and coldness are all a matter of degree.

The same principle also applies to Spirit and Matter; they begin by showing that they are two poles of the same thing – merely intermediate planes varying in degrees of vibration. Just like liquid, ice and gas are three different states of water, they might be water in nature, but their degrees vary.

This overarching principle can also be applied to all the different pairs in the universe, i.e., large and small, positive and negative, light and dark, hard and soft, alive and dead. The mental plane of reality also works on the same principle, such as love and hate, faith and fear, happy and sad. All these opposites are varying degrees of the same emotion. This law is fundamental since it helps one develop the ability to transform the vibrations from one end of the continuum to another. This in essence is known as the study of *"Alchemy."*

Alchemy

In the Middle Age, Alchemists were engrossed with the task of converting base metals into gold. They held a stern belief that alchemy went hand-in-hand with the purity of one's mind, body and spirit; only then would they be able to be successful alchemists.

On a spiritual level, it signifies developing a holistic understanding of your underlying thoughts, feelings, actions and directing your energies into forming soul realized energies into spiritual gold.

Alchemists worked to purify themselves by eliminating the base material of the self, and achieving the gold of self-realization, spiritual freedom, and enlightenment.

What this means, is that your mind has the power to turn feelings of *'hate'* *(metal)* into *'love'(gold)* – just like an Alchemist, you can get your *lower Self* to elevate to your *higher Self*, and you can *ascend* to your light body version from your physical state.

Oneness can be achieved, as opposed to separation, by capitalizing on your mind's polarizing ability and tuning its balance together with your consciousness.

A person who operates by the emotional body needs to become polarized in their mental body. If your mental or intellectual self is the dominant version, you need to be polarized by the soul. Similarly, a person deeply into their soul needs to become polarized to the monad, and someone merged in the monad needs to become more polarized towards God.

In essence, everything possesses polarity. In the absence of the principle of polarity, everything would come to a standstill – even the most potent forces in nature. This will create absolute chaos and disharmony.

The Principle of Polarity equips us with the intellect to make choices when we are presented with the option between right and wrong, good and bad, love and hate, truth and lies, fear and faith, generosity and greed.

It is nature's way of holding what is true to our actions and the choices we make by returning our deeds to us in the way we treated others. *'The principle of cause and effect"* comes into play here and establishes a close connection with polarity, just like the pendulum, which comes back to its original position.

Under the *"Law of Patterns,"* anything whether good or bad, reinforces itself and becomes a part of second nature until we make conscious efforts to break the cycle and do something novel and different.

If the habit is working on positive and beneficial behavior, it is recommended that you continue with it and self-reward yourself to encourage that behavior. By acting spontaneously, we can bring innovation into our lives so that we can build a new framework to lead our lives and mold our behavior accordingly.

This ability to be flexible and versatile is mainly due to the learning habits that we acquire at a young age. Survival values are the learning lessons that we got by observing patterns and fitting in the pieces of the puzzle together. Once we identify the pattern is not beneficial to us, we can get down to correct it by doing things differently, unique, introducing something new, constructive, and positive.

The Principle of Correspondence

"As above, so below, as within, so without, as the universe, so the soul."

-Hermes Trismegistus.

This principle talks about how the energies of the planets and the stars in the heavens are replicated in the energies within humans. It states no separation between different planes of existence (physical, mental, and spiritual). They all exist, manifest, and correspond to each other and to different vibrational levels. According to this law, all three planes vibrate in harmony and agree with each other. There are no divisions between them but degrees on the scale of life. We humans who live below are also bestowed with the same energies found above in the heavens. The universe is referred to as macrocosm and the individual self as the microcosm under this principle.

"We are the gods of the atoms that make up ourselves, but we are also the atoms of the gods that make up the universe,"

- Manly P. Hall.

Our souls being immortal selves belong to the Creator, like the stars found in the heavens. The heavens found among the planets and the stars make up human beings. The comparison is also extended to the chemical energies found in the heavens, namely sodium, sulfur, phosphorous, hydrogen, iron, and magnesium, which also make up living organisms below, as above. A dying star becomes ash that once belonged to the Creator. Similarly, our immortal essence becomes mortal ash.

Although it looks like we are not in a complete state of harmony, our thoughts, words, emotions, and actions will affect the state of harmony we will perceive and experience in life.

You will always be presented with great learning lessons that will help you resolve your Karma, and together what we think, say, feel, and do create the environment in which we operate. If more and more people strive towards establishing peace, we would have a peaceful world to live in. We are all **"ONE"** entity and somehow deeply interconnected and intertwined like the various personalities we keep. It is a matter of great responsibility and something that we all need to understand and accept;

"We are all linked by a mesh of energies that we contain within us."

-Heidi M. Morrison.

Chapter 4: The Self

"The outward freedom that we shall attain will only be in exact proportion to the inward freedom to which we may have grown at a given moment. And if this is a correct view of freedom, our chief energy must be concentrated on achieving reform from within."

–Mahatma Gandhi.

Recapturing Your Self

When was the last time you took time out to connect and reflect on your inner self? How much time do you spend on introspection? This chapter is specifically written to recapture your own essence and to help you start focusing on what lies deep within you.

When we talk about *"the Self,"* it's about how well we align our being into the path to make peace with every part of ourselves, and ultimately become "**Whole.**"

To understand this concept, we must have the awareness that our human energetic anatomy, is made up of five energy layers.

- *Physical Energy*
- *Etheric Energy*
- *Emotional Energy*
- *Mental Energy*

- *Spiritual Energy*

All these layers form the core of who we are, and they are all inextricably linked to each other. The type of relationship that we have with each of these energy bodies is quite significant, as we cannot have a healthy existence without these energy bodies being in harmony. All layers of our energetic bodies are connected to each other, and they affect one another. Thus, we must pay attention and nurture all our energetic bodies with the necessary amount of attention that they require.

Oftentimes, we separate them – focusing on one or two while ignoring the other ones. When we just focus on our physical body and ignore our mental, emotional, and spiritual bodies (or vice versa), we lose our balance. All five layers of our human energy bodies are equally important for our overall wellbeing. As all of them together make you who *'You'* are, as a *'Whole.'*

The apparent outer layer is the physical body that comprises shape, volume, and weight. This is what meets the eye – something tangible that you can touch and see. However, we need to be aware that seven energy layers surround our physical body, comprising of a person's aura. These layers are where our mental, emotional, physical, and spiritual energetic imprints are, and where they get stored.

  o *Physical Energy:* The first layer of our physical body is an amalgamation of flesh, skin, organs, bones, blood, and energy. This is the layer that we consider as our physical selves.
  o *Etheric Energy:* the name comes from the word ether. It is located approximately ¼ to approximately an inch from the

physical body. This layer has been described as quite similar to a spider's web – stretchy and sticky. The etheric energy body has also been referred to as the *"blueprint"* of the physical body. Its shape resembles the physical body.

- **Emotional Energy:** The emotional layer is embedded centrally among the five closest layers of our body aura, and it contains all the imprints of our memories and feelings. This layer has most of the energy and can be quite changeable as it can experience the lows and highs at the end of the continuum.
- **Mental Energy:** Our ideas appear and evolve from this layer and form the belief system that we carry within ourselves. Here is where our thoughts are processed and cemented together and compartmentalized to prioritize what matters and then assign weightage in order of importance. We then proceed to build a perception of the things we see and experience around us.
- **Spiritual Energy:** The last layer of our aura. It is the human energy field layer where our higher awareness and consciousness lie and ultimately extend. This layer paints the final picture of our mental state and helps unite all our past references in connection to '*universal consciousness.*'

"At the core, everything begins with the relationship we have within ourselves. When this relationship doesn't exist (either it is ignored or abandoned) or is not healthy, that is when we start experiencing pain, anxiety, and disease"

-Heidi M. Morrison.

Self-Love

It is the Love of the Self. It is to have an appreciation of one's own **worth** or virtue. It begins with honoring ourselves by focusing on our own feelings, thoughts, words, and actions as if we were our own best friend. *Self-Love* is free of judgment and attachments.

By practicing acceptance, appreciation, understanding, compassion, respect, and forgiveness to yourself, you can achieve self-love.

Self-Love also requires us to have the **integrity** to '*the Self*,' have a purity of heart, and to be honest to ourselves. We attain Self-love once we **reconcile** with all parts of ourselves and become our own best friend. This is possible to achieve if you have the determination, commitment, discipline, and resolution of purpose. In other words, self-love is about finding peace and contentment within '*the Self*,' without relying on social validation, having self-respect, and self-acceptance as you carve out your own integral individuality. Self-love is to Honor yourself, spend time with yourself reading a book, pursue a hobby that makes you happy, take a class that makes your soul grow, or just lay down at the park and enjoy yourself being immersed in nature.

> *"Investing in your own being, nurturing yourself mentally, emotionally, physically, and spiritually – that is Self-love."*
>
> —Heidi M. Morrison.

To love is all about being kind to oneself, other people, and all living things. It is free from any traces of envy, pride, or pretension. It's all about focusing on positivity rather than negativity. Love rejoices with the truth, not finding delight in harm. To love yourself is to accept who you are and embrace your imperfections completely. Do not fall prey to other's negative comments. Be completely sure about yourself that nobody can dim your light and pull you down.

Unconditional Self - Love is the highest version of love. It is the kind of love that *knows* you are loved and lovable. When you love yourself and others in their true form, you are honoring yourself and everyone else's journey to salvation and soul path. Loving without reservation makes us aware that we are a part of God, and we all belong to him. The only time that you connect with your *Higher Self'* is when you love unconditionally and do not expect anything in return.

Unconditional Love helps us be our unapologetic self, and our communication automatically becomes streamlined, and we say the right thing at the right time. Life comes easily to us when we love unconditionally. Suppose you go out of your way to express unconditional love. In that case, you will automatically eliminate your fears and transcend far above them, opening yourself fully to the expression of Unconditional love.

> *"Once your Soul becomes the un-corruptible one, only then, you will have attained a real level of unconditional self-love that no-one can break."*
>
> –Heidi M. Morrison.

We all have the capacity to develop unconditional love within ourselves. *"Allow yourself to see your creator inside you."* Acknowledge your feelings, acknowledge your intuition, and listen to yourself. Once you learn and allow to love yourself unconditionally, you will feel empowered and in control of your life.

Remember! You have the choice to filter your emotions, thoughts, words, and actions as they determine your well-being.

-Heidi M. Morrison.

Begin by *accepting yourself* for who you are. *Acceptance* is integral in growing into a more refined, polished, and beautiful version of yourself. Many people keep running after an image of themselves that others have formed or some standard that society sets for them. It is important to move your attention from other people towards yourself, focusing your attention on investigating and finding what you like and dislike, how powerful and incredible you are.

"By focusing all our energies on ourselves and working on becoming better human beings, the world will be a better place to live for all of us."

-Heidi M. Morrison.

The entire process of healing helped me find my true self and regain my perspective on life. One night, my Akashic Records teacher gave me an assignment to *'Writer a Letter to my Soul.'* As I lay on my bed about to sleep, I placed my hands on the center of my chest and breathed deeply, communicating a message to my soul. I fell asleep, only to be woken up later by three knocks on my heart center. I was surprised but, at the same time, aware of my intention. So, I intentionally opened the door of my heart. I could hear and see a little baby crying. Addressing the baby, I asked her why she was crying, to which she replied, *"I want my Mommy."* At that moment, I realized that this little baby girl was my inner child – my Soul. That night, I cried like a baby. My heart cried because I had ignored my inner child for a very long time.

That is when I understood that self-love is all about honoring your true feelings, inner truth, hard-core beliefs, and intuition. It's all about validating your intuition without letting other people's opinions influence you or your thought process. I apologize to my soul for not being there for the baby inside me. The day I wrote a letter to my soul for this purpose, I felt amazing and filled my heart with immense joy. It felt like being reunited with my best friend.

Practice

- *Open your heart to your Soul today. "Write a letter to your Soul."*

- *Begin by placing your hands on your Heart Chakra (center of your chest) breathing deeply in and out unconditional love, compassion, and acceptance.*
- *Once you start feeling these emotions inside your heart; - expand them into every cell, atom, and organ of your entire being.*
- *Now, you are ready to write a letter to your Soul.*
- *Great Job!*

Besides respecting your beliefs, values, and intuitions, it is equally important to take **'responsibility'** and own up to your feelings, as there is no point evading and running from them so that you can re-connect and make peace with your own self - Your own Soul point of balance. This attunement with our hearts is the **'all and the everything'** of who we are.

> "Knowledge of the self is the root of all knowledge."
>
> –Heidi M. Morrison.

Practice

These are steps I found to be useful during my journey towards Self-love:

1. **Pay attention to your Inner Voice:** Start by paying attention to how you are treating yourself. Some people often have a conversation with themselves in their minds, but they are unaware of it. First, observe, then identify, without

judgment, what your inner voice is trying to tell you. Have you been ignoring your inner voice lately? The more positive you are about yourself and your personality, you will be able to do something amazing for yourself and your life. Be mindful of what you tell yourself every time you make a mistake. Do you beat yourself up about it? If you can love yourself at times when things are difficult, then you will pass this test.

2. *Take Control of your Inner Voice:* There are certain things that you have been fed your whole life, whether it is by family, friends, or society. You might not consciously pay attention to it, but it is important to know that over time, these thoughts start to metamorphose themselves into your mind and become a part of your personality – and destiny. Often, these messages in your head are not what the truth is. To have a clear understanding and vision of what is really happening, you need to get out of the turmoil and rise above the clutter and noise that could be surrounding you, creating blind spots around your aura that will not allow you to see the truth and what is really happening.

3. *Becoming Neutral:* By becoming a neutral observer, all those negative thoughts that once bombarded your mind vanish, as you start observing yourself without judgment and understanding.

All this is possible with practice. Tell yourself, *"I love you"* every time you look at yourself in the mirror. Acknowledge your greatness and appreciate every part of your being. Be grateful for everything that you are and have in your life. Say **"Thank you"** to yourself for being your own support system day in and day out.

"Remember who you are at the deepest level of your Soul, as you embrace the Light and Love of God within you."

-Heidi M. Morrison.

Practice

- *Reprogram your Self-love today!*
- *Repeat each one of the following affirmations 3 to 5 times every day.*

"I Am Acceptance"

"I Accept Myself Just as I Am"

"I Am Love"

"I Love Myself Just as I Am"

"I Am Forgiveness"

"I Forgive Myself to The Deepest Level of My Soul"

"I Allow Myself to Give Love"

"I Allow Myself to Receive Love"

"I Am Lovable"

Chapter 5: Karma

"The first step to free yourself from Karma is to forgive yourself from the depths of your Soul."

–Heidi M. Morrison.

"Karma" is the Sanskrit word for action. It is equivalent to Newton's law, *"every action has a reaction."* All our thoughts, what-ifs, how we speak, and act, are strengthened by a synchronous force within our internal processes – Karma. This law holds the fact in high regard that the phenomenon of cause and effect does exist. We cannot escape the natural forces of Karma by ignoring our thoughts and actions. Know that *ignorance* will not save you, or me, from continuously creating Karma in our life. Every one of us is accountable for how we think, speak, act, and react. The gift of *intelligence* is what differentiates us from other living beings, such as animals and plants. We are also given the **power of choice** and **free will,** and we must ingrain these thoughts and practices into our personalities so that we do not suffer at the hands of Karma.

To understand this concept holistically, we must consider every cell in our human body as a library of energy and information. As we mentioned before in a previous chapter, '*We*' and the '*Whole Universe*' are mainly composed of water molecules, and it is scientifically proven that water carries energy and information.

It is essential to understand that we all branch out from the same energy source. These energetic frequencies and vibrations interconnect the entire human race with the universe. No separation classifies people into different categories. Nothing can separate you as an entity distinct from the air, water, trees, plants, animals, and other things that make up your surroundings and the ecosystem.

Whether we are consciously aware of it or not, we all derive energies from each other. Be it beneficial or not, we not only carry our *own Karma*, but we also share *personal Karmas*, *cultural Karmas*, and even *inherited Karmas* that get the entire human race involved – also known as **collective Karma**. All these Karmas must co-exist in mutual peace and harmony as they are dependent on each other. Whatever life sends your way, and whatever you experience, form a mesh of all the Karmas interacting one with another to create an experience of sorts. If you give all this some focused thought, you will realize that Karma is a consequence of a non-love place, pouring in your thoughts, speech, actions and re-action. Unity always comes from a place of love, while judgment and separation come from a place of non-love. **Forgiveness** is a form of unconditional love, which, in turn, leads to wholeness. Once we become whole, we heal.

> *"Forgiveness is something that can hold the entire universe together as a Whole."*
>
> *–Heidi M. Morrison.*

As a universal human fraternity, it is important to understand that we are all causality of the same disease. If all of us make individual efforts on our part, together, we will make this world a better place.

"By taking responsibility and playing our role in imparting the gift of forgiveness and love to ourselves and to the world, we will start liberating ourselves from all pain and suffering, and gift ourselves with Peace and Spiritual Freedom."

–Heidi M. Morrison.

Affirm 3 times:

"Today, I will practice compassion, gentleness, and understanding to myself and to others."

'**Buddha**' believed that Karma brings together all our thoughts, words, and actions into implementation in the form of others performing under our instructions. *This doctrine was explained by Shatapatha Brahmana:*

"While our bodies may die, the soul is eternal, and it continues its journey through many lifetimes. The soul creates a system of actions and reactions (Karma) throughout these lives, forming a cycle of rebirth. And the totality of our actions and their reactions

in this and previous lives determine our future. Thus — a man is born to the world he has made."

- Shatapatha Brahmana.

The Law of Karma

The Great *"Law of Cause and Effect"* is something that everyone inherently knows and understands. The famous saying, *"As you sow, so shall you reap,"* is common knowledge nowadays. Without getting an in-depth understanding of this concept, we will never fully grasp the concept of *"Dharma"* or undertake the journey on the spiritual path.

The law of Karma is not a straightforward concept and requires considerable understanding and profound analysis. Since the law of cause and effect forms the very basis of Karma, it goes unsaid that everything happens according to certain laws. When these laws are not acknowledged, we tend to give it the name of chance. No phenomenon on this planet escapes the *"Law of Cause and Effect,"* as everything that happens around you has a reason and logical explanation behind it. All walks of life are governed by specific laws, and we can never negate them in any way. If we were to track down each chain link of causation, we would inevitably find out that every link has a beginning and an end that originates in the non-physical or spiritual world.

"You are what your deep, driving desire is. As your desire is, so is your will. As your will is, so is your deed (Karma). As your deed (Karma) is, so is your destiny."

—*Brihadaranyaka Upanishad.*

As powerful human beings that we are, the law of Karma reminds us to *"use our power wisely,"* as for every action, there will be a reaction.

Every little thought that crosses your mind and every decision that you make – followed by an action – sparks a series of unseen chains of cause and effect. These vibes of causations emanate from the mental plane and transcend into every cell and atom of our body. It finally exudes into our surroundings; whose effects go as far as the cosmos. As the pendulum swings back to its starting place, the vibratory energy finds its way back to where it originated. All these series of actions happen in the blink of an eye. Causations are known to occur in almost seven dimensions of reality. Commonly, we do not have the supreme knowledge or understanding to comprehend and digest the reasons for these effects.

The purpose of directing our energies and trying to understand the Universal Laws is to make sure that we do not accumulate unnecessary Karma on our personal accounts – *"Akashic Records."*

This law is mathematically or mechanically operative. As per the karmic law, every human is bound to find ultimate peace, contentment and fulfillment.

> *"What binds man to the re-incarnational wheel is Karma. Karma accumulates in places where attachments and personal ego exist and festers."*
>
> –Heidi M. Morrison.

You must understand that you have so much power within you to create not only good experiences but also bad ones. If you are not careful of the kind of energy that you allow in your life, your thoughts and actions will inevitably cause pain and suffering to yourself and others. Human beings often make uninformed, ignorant, and selfish choices without considering other people's wellbeing, resulting in the accumulation of bad Karma. When we get so immersed in our material, worldly lives, we cannot undertake our lives' most important educational journey –towards Spiritual Freedom. This causation of fear can only be eliminated from our lives once we take responsibility for acquiring the knowledge, understanding, and wisdom of all Universal Spiritual Laws.

Forgiveness

Forgiveness is what starts the journey to a more fulfilling life. Forgiveness comes with its fair share of struggles and becomes more challenging to implement as it gives off the impression that the transgressor would be forgiven once and for all and put an end to the matter. However, forgiveness does not mean that the wrongdoer of the transgression – no matter how small or big – is absolved. The person still owns up to it and will have to take responsibility for their actions.

> *"Only through forgiveness can the human race continue their legacy."*
>
> –Heidi M. Morrison.

To forgive is an act that releases previously accumulated anger and allows the ***"Law of Grace"*** to dispense and intercede with the Karma any person has stored in their Akasha. When you learn to forgive out of love, it helps you grow spiritually and regain spiritual freedom. It is essential to become aware that compassion, understanding, and non-violence are the natural outgrowth of the law of forgiveness.

Forgiving is a holy trait, and this graceful trait of forgiveness binds the universe together. Forgiveness represents eternal virtue and is a supreme quality that an individual can possess.

> *"Forgiveness is the cornerstone that enables all other virtues. Without having the capacity to forgive, incarnating other virtues simply could not be possible."*
>
> – Heidi M. Morrison.

Becoming Non-Attach

> *"Attachments to the self-and/or others, give birth to Karma."*
>
> –Heidi M. Morrison.

Non-attachment is the key to weaken its effects. When an individual realizes that the ultimate nature of the Self is *empty*, then they will achieve a state of non-attachment.

The Self that we get so attached to, resides within us, and is not a separate entity. To liberate yourself from the self's attachment, you must attain a complete conceptual understanding of this law. Two main methods have been chosen for helping human beings achieve this realization and liberation, one known as spiritual practice and the other non-attached behavior.

Taking Responsibility

Responsibility means to have the ability to respond. You must own your thoughts, actions, reactions and have this deeply embedded in your value system that whatever happens to you throughout your journey, is the result of your actions, as well as the way you have reacted. Nobody is to be blamed for your issues. Your life is a reflection of your deeds and actions.

Whether your life takes an upward trajectory, or a downturn is entirely your responsibility. This karmic law makes you realize that you need to develop an *'internal locus of control'* rather than an external one. By creating an internal locus of control, you hold yourself responsible for rectifying and fixing the loopholes that need amendment. Alongside this, learn to identify, recognize, and establish the boundaries that define your degree of responsibility. Only then, you can wholly take responsibility for your actions and let go of things that are not.

Free Will

Under the effect of the third dimension, the human mind and soul have the right to bring their creative and expressive energies into the world – both negatively and positively. This is our final decision, and we have the right to contract or expand. Irrespective of the situation prevailing around us, as an individual, *you have the power to choose the direction of your life.* We might get inspired by others or try to follow their example. Whatever the reason is, remember, your mind is the builder, and your thoughts are a product of your mind. We all have *"Free Will."*

Goodwill

Goodwill is best described by this quote -

"A goodwill is good not because of what its effects, or accomplishes, not because of its fitness to attain some intended end, but good just by its willing, i.e., in itself; and, considered by itself, it is to be esteemed beyond compare much higher than anything that could ever be brought about by it in favor of some inclinations, and indeed, if you will, the sum of all inclinations. Nothing can possibly be conceived in the world, or even out of it, which can be called good, without qualification, except a good will."

–Immanuel Kant.

Chapter 6: Breathing

"Breath is the bridge which connects life to consciousness, which unites your body to your thoughts. Whenever your mind becomes scattered, use your breath as the means to take hold of your mind again."

–Thich Nhat Hanh.

Breathing freely and fully is our birthright. The day we incarnated into this world, we take our first breath, and the day we die, our last. In essence, each breath we take is a continuous process of getting energy from the Universe, and then returning it. With each inhale, we take in life, and with each exhale, we return it back to the Universe – creating the essential *flow of life.*

As we become aware and make a conscious effort to work with our breath, it establishes a direct link to our autonomic nervous system, gaining access to a part of our bodies that usually works independent of our conscious awareness.

Mindfulness exercises, breathing and relaxation techniques, such as yoga, meditation and breathwork, make use of this innate ability to focus on our breath. The benefits that our breath has on our mind and body are innumerable. When we consciously focus and practice appropriate and controlled breathing, several regions in the brain get activated. All of them linked to attention, thought processing, creativity, imagination, intuition, emotions, memories, body awareness and our senses (vision, speech, touch, hearing and smell).

Our Breath works as a cleanser, pushing all energetic blockages we might have in our body, chakras, and aura. Breathing helps us connect and release mental and emotional stagnant energetic pain that is stuck in our physical body. It helps decrease feelings of stress and anxiety while relaxing our muscles, boosting our immune system, stabilizing our blood pressure, and increasing all energetic levels in our body and mind. Additionally, our breath gives us the opportunity to open the door that connects us with our own essence – our Soul – and aligns us with the energy of the Universe, the Unified Field.

All breathing techniques are incredibly effective. I have learned and practice different breathing techniques, but from time to time, one breathing technique will work better for me than the others. There is no formula to follow; I listen to my own self, identify what I need and want at that specific moment, and together with the knowledge of the existing breathing techniques, I utilize the one that will fit better for the time and space I am in.

Modalities of Breathing

Mindful Breathing

This form of breathing involves being aware and mindful of your breath, focusing all your attention on it. As you consciously feel the air going in and out of your lungs, nose, or mouth, and flowing all throughout your being, with your mind, you can control your breathing pattern, telling your breath to slow down, and as you slow down, this will help you clear your mind and relax your whole being from within.

Practice

- *Start with 5 to 7 minutes a day (set up your timer).*
- *Find a comfortable position, either sitting down on a chair or lying flat on your back and close your eyes.*
- *Begin by taking a deep breath, in through your nose, and breathing out through your nose.*
- *As you continue breathing nice and slow, focus your attention on your senses. Feel what you feel, notice what you notice; just observe your breath without judgment.*
- *As you observe your breath, you can modify your breathing patterns and direct your energy to different areas of your body, accustoming it to your own needs and wants.*
- *This process must be done effortlessly and joyfully.*

Remember!
"To breathe is vital and your birth right, not a chore."

Mantra Breathing

This form of breathing uses the **'power of words'** to reinforce a particular belief in your mind.

Mantras have this extraordinary power to focus all your attention on the task at hand, as they also work as a way to re-program yourself, bringing your mind and body into a positive and relaxed state.

Practice

- *Find a calm, comfortable place, and position yourself laying down flat on your back, sitting down on a chair, or even standing.*
- *Start by breathing slowly in and out, following a tempo.*
- *Choose a positive word or phrase; let's say, '****Peace*** *'or '****I AM Peace.****'*
- *Repeat the word or phrase as you continue breathing nice and slow – in and out for about 5 to 7 minutes.*
- *As you feel reinvigorated with an energy of peace, expand this energy all around you.*

Focal Breathing

This form of breathing makes use of **'*visualization'*** to create a focal point of attention into your breath.

As you inhale, visualize one side of a square in your mind. When you're done doing one side, you repeat the process to get your mind to imagine the other side of the square. This helps shift your energy, calm down your nervous system, connect you to the depth of your physical body, de-stress your body, and release tension.

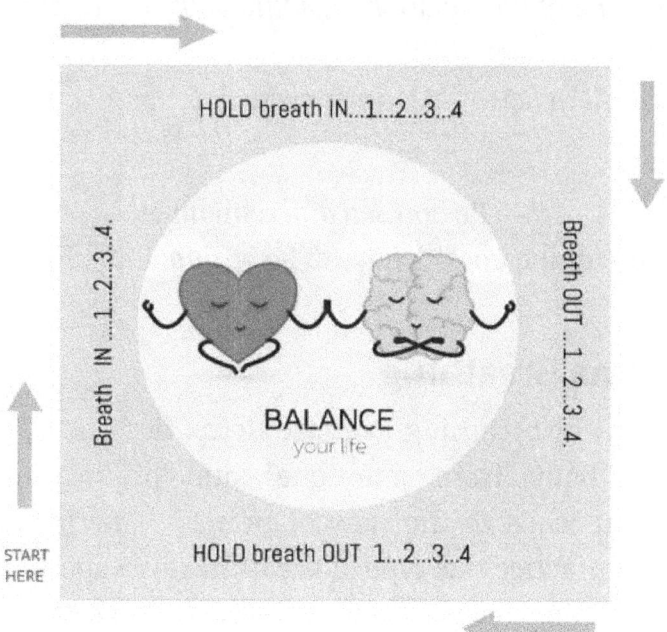

Practice

- *Start by sitting down on a chair, place your feet flat on the ground, place your hands palms up on your lap, and close your eyes.*
- *Imagine a square, make it of your favourite colour and notice its four sides.*
- *Start from the bottom left corner, counting 1,2,3,4 as you trace one side of the square with your breath and inner eye. Then, count 1,2,3,4 as you hold your breath and trace the topside of the square, count 1,2,3,4 as you continue tracing down the right side of the square with your breath, and then finish tracing the*

bottom line of the square by holding your breath and counting 1,2,3,4.
- Repeat this at least 3 to 5 times every day.

Be amused and remember!
"Breathing doesn't have to be boring; it can be FUN!"

Pranayama Breathing

This form of breathing exercise detoxifies and clears your mind and body from emotional and physical energetic blockages. It leads to the flow of prana – *'life force energy.'* People who practice this type of breathing are supercharged!

This breathing technique is believed to have the power to clean 72,000 channels in your body. Once these channels open, a sense of liberation fills your entire self, and you are charged to the highest degree. They are many different forms of Pranayama breathing. The one I refer to here involves inhaling deeply twice through your mouth and then exhaling deeply once through your mouth.

Practice

- *Lay down flat on your back, arm on your side, palms open facing up, and close your eyes.*
  - *Begin taking your first breath through your mouth, filling up your belly (imagine as if you have a big balloon inside). Inhale again through your mouth, this time filling up your*

heart center (raising your chest), and then exhale all thru your mouth as you empty and deflate your belly.
- *Start with 3 to 5 minutes a day.*
- *Once you are done breathing this way, finish by breathing through your nose for another minute or two, or as needed.*

Nostril Breathing

It is a yogic breath control practice. It entails closing one part of your nostril and taking in the air slowly through the other nostril. It helps to reduce anxiety and agitation as it **'balances'** your brain drastically. This form of breathing has a profound settling impact on the body, mind, and emotions.

Practice

- *Starting with your right hand, place your right thumb on your right nostril and your ring and little fingers on your left nostril.*
- *Begin by closing off your right nostril, breathing slowly and deeply through your left nostril only.*
- *Now, close both nostrils and hold your breath. Exhale through the right nostril (repeat 3 to 5 times).*
- *Once you finish with that side, switch to the other side. Switch hands.*
- *Place your left thumb on your left nostril and your ring and little fingers on your right, closing off your left nostril, breathing slowly and deeply through your right nostril.*
- *Now, close both sides and hold your breath. Exhale through the left nostril (Repeat 3 to 5 times).*

- *What do you notice? How do you feel?*

Belly Breathing

This form of breathing initiates from your belly. As you inhale, you fill up your belly with air – like a balloon. As you exhale, you deflate this metaphoric balloon.

Practice

- *Relax your body by lying flat on your back or sitting comfortably on a chair.*
- *Place the palms of your hands on your abdomen and begin by taking a deep belly breath in through your nose, feeling your abdomen expanding and rising as the air goes inside your body, and then exhale all the air out through your mouth. Notice your abdomen contracting as the air starts to move out of your lungs.*

"The way you breathe is the way you live. Breathing is essential to life and necessary for good health."

–Heidi M. Morrison.

Moving into the Present Moment

To be Present and to live in the Here and Now is to have all our energies focused on what is happening in that specific moment. It shifts our attention to the center of our being and helps us flow easily in life. To accomplish this requires awareness and mindfulness. Breathing exercises help us find that center.

Practice

Start by sitting down in a chair with your feet flat on the ground, place the palm of your hands on your lap, and close your eyes.

1. Put your attention to the area between your eyebrows and go **"deeper"** – behind your eyes, toward the center of your head.
2. Imagine your whole head is a room; look inside and notice how you have decorated it. Take your time and observe. If it is dark in there and you want to add light, **"create"** a lamp and light switch with your imagination and turn on the light.
3. Notice if someone besides you is inside this room. If so, tell everyone to please leave your room.
4. Start cleaning all the clutter you have in there. Use your imagination!
5. Now, notice a chair in the center of the room. This chair has your name on it.
6. Sit down on that chair. It belongs to YOU and ONLY YOU!

   This is;

   "The BOSS chair"

   "The CEO chair"

   "The DRIVER seat"

"The PRESENT Time chair"
"Congratulation! You made it!"

As you "RECLAIM" your seat, Affirm (3 to 5 times)

"I AM CENTER"

"I AM PRESENT"

"I AM the BOSS of my BEING"

"I AM LIVING in the HERE and the NOW"

This process begins by observing your mind without judgment and taking the appropriate action, intending to return to *the neutral* – your internal still point. When you are in a **neutral state,** you detach yourself of any expectations from the outcome and notice the unbiased reality. Being neutral doesn't mean that you are to be selfish or have a non-caring attitude. It is an act of accepting your surroundings the way they are without taking sides.

When we become a neutral observer, we are learning and cultivating discernment, free from any misunderstandings and confusions, flexible and open-minded. Just like meditation helps cultivate a sense of tranquility, improves focus, and builds clarity; similarly, being neutral is all about breaking free from the clutches of your attachments and learning to *"let go."*

> *"By training our mind to learn to observe, we start moving into a higher level of consciousness and remember who we truly are – deep at the level of our Soul."*
>
> –Heidi M. Morrison.

Meditative breathing techniques and practices teach our body and mind to let go and find their center as we move back into the present moment. When you focus on your breathing, you silence your mind and eliminate the unwanted inner chatter. Distractions will no longer keep you away from achieving your true potential. Your mind becomes calmer and clear with feelings of happiness, contentment, and inner peace.

When you are consciously at peace with yourself through breathing and meditation, you open yourself up to a plethora of opportunities. It will help anchor you into the present moment and connect you with your inner and outer world.

> *"Breathing is the centerpiece of Meditation. Honor yourself and breathe today"*
>
> –Heidi M. Morrison.

Meditation is the art of developing relationship with your breath that brings focus, balance, and peace of mind. It is always available for you from the moment you are born till you die. Your breath is like your brain's remote control. Focusing your attention on your breath can manually help you alter your state of consciousness. The way you breathe in a given moment, is an absolute reflection of your thought process. It teaches us the invaluable lesson of letting go, just as we exhale, releasing tension and non-beneficial energies that are in our brain and body. At the same time as we breathe in, our breath teaches us the lesson of receiving unconditional life force from the universe – to feel Joy and to be grateful for being alive.

"Meditation is a universal practice, and our breath is a universal language."

-Heidi M. Morrison.

Chapter 7: Energetic Anatomy

Root Chakra — Basic Trust
Sacral Chakra — Sexuality, Creativity
Solar Plexus — Wisdom, Power
Heart Chakra — Love, Healing
Throat Chakra — Communication
Third Eye — Awareness
Crown Chakra — Spirituality

"The foundation of success in life is good health: that is the substratum fortune; it is also the basis of happiness. A person cannot accumulate a fortune very well when he is sick."

–P. T. Barnum.

If you ever have attended a Yoga class, Reiki session, Sound bath, Breathwork, Meditation class, or any other type of energetic healing modality, it is most likely that you have heard about **the Chakras, the Aura, the Meridians** and even words like **Prana, Chi, Ki,** or **Life Force Energy.**

Let's define all these concepts before we expound on this subject.

"Life force" is the vital principle or animating force that exists within all living beings. Life force energy is what keeps us alive and healthy. The difference between a healthy person and an ill

person is their quality and quantity of Life Force Energy flowing in, through and around their energy body.

In Japan, they called it *'Ki'*, the Taoists call it *'Chi,'* or *'Qi'*, and in India, they call it *'Prana.'* Christians referred to it as *'The Light'* or *'The Holy Ghost'* and many other cultures and religions worldwide have named it differently. However, they all refer to the same **"Life Force Energy."** This flow of Life Force Energy is vital because it directly affects the well-functioning of all our organs and systems in our bodies.

We have discovered that we not only have a physical anatomy, but we also have an energetic anatomy. To fully utilize the seven Chakras, it is essential to have a basic understanding of our body's energetic anatomy and why it is so necessary for our well-being.

Energetic Anatomy

Our energetic anatomy is a network of energy inside and around our body. It contains our energy fields – *'Aura,'* power centers – *'Chakras,'* and passageways – *'Meridians.'* These interlock within our physical body and affect all our energy bodies (mental, emotional, physical, spiritual, and etheric). To develop a better understanding, let's divide our energetic anatomy into three major categories.

- **The Chakras** - Chakras are energetic *processing centers* located inside our bodies. They regulate and maintain energy and information from your physical, emotional, mental, and spiritual bodies.

- **The Meridians** -These are the *energy channels* in our bodies responsible for transferring life force between the Chakras in synchrony with the surrounding organs and the other parts of our body.
- **The Aura** -They are also referred to as your *subtle body*. The Aura originates from inside the Chakras and radiates from the body's pores, expanding in every direction around the physical body.

We have seven main layers of Aura, well-nestled within one another, like a set of seven Russian dolls – each one inside the other. Every layer originates from one Chakra in our body. We find the first layer of our Aura at the edge of our physical body. It originates from the first Chakra, the Root or Base Chakra. The second layer runs on top of the first layer and originates at the Sacral Chakra – the second energy center. This continues all the way to the seventh and last layer that forms from the seventh energy center or the Crown Chakra. All the layers of our Aura follow a concentric circular pattern, like the layers of an onion. The Aura is the place where our memories, events, trauma, and impressions (pictures and information) get stored.

The Chakra System

There are seven main Chakras that lie along our spine. Every Chakra can be identified with a specific name, color, number, and a particular location. They are responsible for gathering energy and information from our surroundings. They then process it internally and express it out into the universe.

> *"Having your Chakras 'open and balanced' will allow you to access higher states of consciousness, release emotional blockages, and achieve overall well-being."*
>
> *–Heidi M. Morrison.*

Ancient yogis taught us the locations of these seven Chakras thousands of years ago. Still now, with modern science, it is found that these seven major Chakras correspond to seven central nerve ganglia located on our spinal column. Each of these nerve bundles influences the energy body we call Aura, as well as our physical body. This area cannot be seen or felt by physical means, but it can be perceived with our Extra Sensorial Perceptions (ESP), spiritual, psychic-body, and psychic-eye.

As your aura expands, this is where your energy flows until it reaches the edge of your energy field and starts connecting with the Unified Field. When energy is not flowing correctly in our body, the Chakras will most likely get blocked. This means that the energy flowing into different parts of our body will become constrained. This energy blockage will most likely lead to mental, emotional, and physical triggers that in turn, will be manifested as anxiety, poor digestion, lethargy, and other health problems.

The Endocrine System and the Chakras

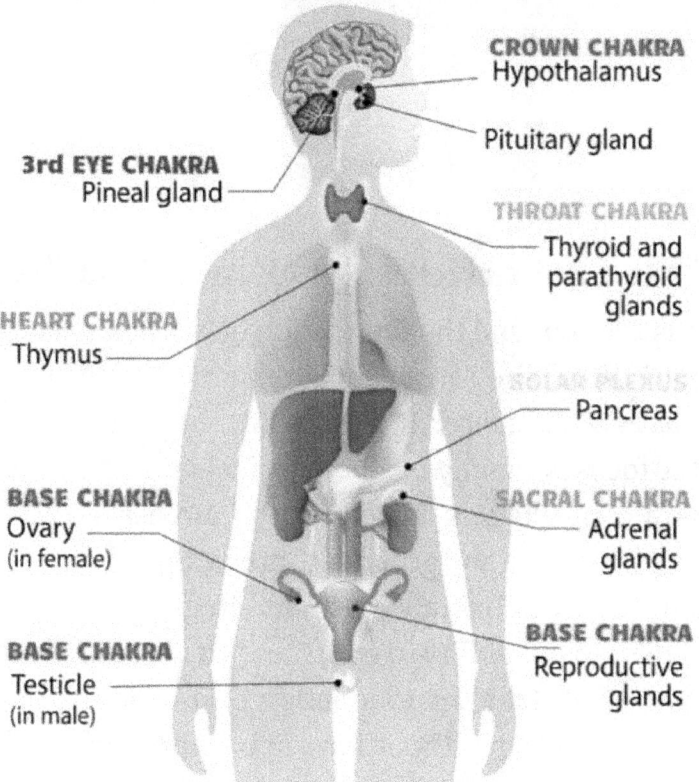

1. Base Chakra (Sanskrit Name: Muladhara)

It is the root and the foundation of all the Chakra systems in our bodies. The Sanskrit meaning of *"Muladhara"* is *'root and basis of Existence.'* It is found at the base of your spine, and it focuses mainly on the physical body. The Muladhara Chakra connects you directly with *"Mother Earth,"* helping you stay centered and grounded, providing a feeling of safety. When the Root Chakra is open and in good balance, we feel confident in our ability to withstand challenges and stand on our own feet. Like the foundation of a building, our bodies cannot be strong without having a strong Root Chakra. As humans, our Base Chakra is the most important and primordial Chakra to be developed. It provides holistic support for mental, emotional, and physical health, as well as spiritual health.

Affirmation – Mantra

"I AM"

As you start creating a relationship with *"Mother Earth,"* spending more time in nature, you will learn to utilize its energy. Hug a tree, walk barefoot, lay down on the grass, feel the earth underneath, feel the unconditional love that radiates from her into you. Breathe in deeply, and say, *"thank you"* to Mother Earth – she will never abandon you. She has been here and will continue to be here for you.

Create a relationship with her the same way you create relationships with people you love. Plant a tree, recycle, eat healthy (organic food), take care of the air, drink clean-purified water, breathe, exercise, and take care of your body.

Our Root Chakra represents our physical identity and our interaction with the physical world around us. These include our home, our work, the environment, our body, and even our finances. Every Chakra connects to an anatomical function of our body, and this one is no different. The Root Chakra relates to several bodily functions involved with the reproductive organs, our immune system, digestive system, lymphatic and skeletal systems, fight-and-flight response, and our lower extremities, hips, legs, knees, ankles, feet, and toes. When a person has this Chakra healthy and balanced, it will provide them with foundation and stability – something we all need in order to live a happy, healthy, and prosperous life.

> *"Developing and balancing your Root Chakra will help you prepare for the journey ahead, supporting you in all of life's ups and downs."*
>
> *–Heidi M. Morrison.*

Overactive and Underactive First Chakra

A Chakra can be both overactive and under-active; maintaining its balance is an art. When it's **overactive**, we're bound to have feelings of anger – for no reason. Addictions such as alcoholism, workaholism, drug abuse, compulsive exercising, excessive eating, over-activity, sex-holism, self-absorbedness, and narcissism will flourish. Over time, this will contribute to an unhealthy and unhappy life.

On the other hand, when it is **under-active**, we may feel like we're moving in and out of life. We might experience a short concentration span or simply feel like our *'head is in the clouds'* (what I like to call *"being in la-la-land"*). Under-activity of this Chakra could also be experienced as a resistance to change. Attributes such as hoarding, greediness, feeling ungrounded, instability, and insecurities will grow. Nervousness and worrying will increase ten-folds, and our self-esteem will decrease. We will lack confidence. Self-doubts will manifest, passivity, poor focus, no discipline, lack of drive and stamina, lack of enthusiasm, lethargy, laziness, and fears will appear. Anxiety and disconnection from our physical body will occur, as all of these will plague our body and mind.

These symptoms are due to the fact our survival instincts are affected and disturbed, and our most highlighted sentiment is fear. **'Fear'** is what we call the demon of this Chakra. This fear's role is to keep us alive. However, the problem is when this Chakra is not in good balance, we start to feel threatened even when there is no reason for us to be. On a physical level, we might also face problems with digestion, lower back, hips, legs, knees, ankles, and feet. In some cases, it even could cause ovarian cysts in females and prostate issues in men.

If this Chakra gets compromised through trauma, we might find it challenging to ground ourselves. In this case, I recommend you to intentionally focus more on strengthening and balancing this chakra, guided with the tools I am providing you in this book, you can gain additional help by finding someone who can help you – a professional bodyworker, exercise specialist, or a well-trained energy worker.

Healthy and Balance First Chakra

If your Base-Root Chakra is balanced, you will feel grounded, like a strong oak tree. You will feel safe, secure, and will be prosperous. You will be able to live in the here and now, being able to enjoy the moment. You will also enjoy good physical health and feel comfortable in your own body.

Conclusion

- **Location:** Base of the spine, or coccyx, the perineum (between the anus and genitals), large intestines, reproductive organs, bladder, lower extremities (legs, ankles, feet), immune system, lymph system, skeletal system (teeth and bones).
- **Corresponding gland:** Reproductive

- **Focus:** Stability, the dwelling place of primal energy (kundalini). Associated with instinct, survival, financial independence, money, food, shelter, feeling safe and secure in the world, physical health, the right to be, and to be alive. It is also associated with taking action.
- **Color:** Bright- electric red.
- **Sense:** Smell.
- **Verb – Mantra:** "I Am."
- **Element:** Earth.
- **Age of development:** Between the ages of 1-7.
- **Demons of this Chakra:** Worries and fears.

Practice

- *Focus your attention towards your First Chakra, inside the base of your spine*
- *Imagine a bright red, spinning tornado coming out from your physical body, expanding outwards; into your legs and feet, entering the ground, moving deeper and deeper, through the mantles of Mother Earth, for at least, 10 miles down the surface – connecting you with the core of Mother Earth.*
- *Affirm 3 to 5 times every day.*

   "I AM Grounded"

   "I AM Rooted"

"I AM Safe"

"I AM Present"

"I AM Healthy"

"I AM Prosperous"

"I AM Success"

"I AM Worthy"

"I AM Supported"

"I AM Strong"

"I AM Manifestation"

"I AM Life"

"I AM Releasing all Fears and Worries"

"I HAVE the right to be Here in the World"

"I AM Worthy of all the good Life have to offer"

2. Sacral Chakra (Sanskrit name: Svādhisthāna)

The *Sacral Chakra* is located above the spleen, in the lumbar region, around 2 to 3 inches below the navel. It extends into the middle/lower abdomen, pelvis, kidneys, bladder, reproductive system, sexual organs and even in our bones. The Sanskrit meaning of *"Svādhisthāna"* is one's own home, or individual center of pleasure, passion, and joy. This Chakra is known as **the Seat of Life.** Svādhisthāna is a link between the male and female aspects, between the Sun and the Moon. While the Base Chakra gives you a stable foundation for exploration, the second, Sacral Chakra, is the link between experiencing the world with our senses and enjoying it with our emotions and feelings.

Affirmation – Mantra

"I Feel."

This Chakra represents *reproduction,* the survival of the species, birth, and creation of the new. This is not only limited just to us human beings, but also extends toward all living beings. *Water* is the element that connects us with this Chakra.

Our Sacral Chakra focuses on fluidity, flexibility, emotions, creativity, life changes, movement, transformation, sensuality, and sexuality. Our Sacral Chakra's emphasis on overcoming fear, change, and focusing on enjoyment and pleasurable sensations. On a deeper level, this Chakra is the seat of the *'individual and collective unconscious.'* It is the center of our most primitive and deep-rooted instincts. By purifying this center, the animalistic nature is transcended.

Overactive and Underactive Second Chakra

If the Sacral Chakra is *overactive,* our much-deserved pleasure transforms into addiction, gluttony, and lust. Satisfying our sexual urges is a primal need, but when we start enjoying it in an unhealthy way and continuously succumb to these primal urges, we disrupt the balance. This may lead to many different addictions, such as excessive sugar intake, obesity, hormone imbalances, restlessness, alcohol intake, unhealthy relationships, and little to no personal boundaries. When *under-active,* we are bound to feel depressed. There is a decrease in sexual performance and eventually, a lack of passion, creativity, and little empathy. We may also suffer from low self-esteem, mood swings, and become unable to let go and move on with our lives. Creativity is risky endeavor mainly due to the fact whenever we do anything out of the ordinary/different, we make ourselves vulnerable. You must understand that this vulnerability is a strength, not a weakness. When we are vulnerable, we open ourselves to new experiences and enjoy opportunities for growth.

Healthy and Balanced Second Chakra

If your Sacral Chakra is balanced, you will be able to embrace change and experience a high degree of emotional intelligence. You will have healthy boundaries, be more creative, experience sexual satisfaction, feel passionate about the things you do, and develop the ability to nurture yourself and others. It will become easy to let go and go with the flow. You will be able to surrender to the outcome, be more receptive, empathic, intuitive, self-aware, and be able to honor relationships.

Conclusion

- **Location:** Mid/lower abdomen, pelvis (2-3 inches below the navel), kidneys, bladder, reproductive system, sexual organs, lymph system, nose, and bones.
- **Corresponding gland:** Adrenal.
- **Focus:** Self-creation and expression, self-gratification, creativity, desire, intuition, empathy, sensuality, self-esteem, emotions, and feelings.
- **Color:** Bright- electric orange.
- **Sense:** Taste.
- **Verb- Mantra:** "I Feel."
- **Element:** Water.
- **Age of development:** Between the ages of 8-14.
- **Demons of this Chakra:** Anger, greed, jealousy, guilt.

Practice

- *Focus your attention towards your Second Chakra, mid-lower abdomen.*
- *Imagine a bright orange, spinning tornado coming out from the front and back of your sacral' chakra physical body, expanding outward into your aura.*
- *Affirm 3 to 5 times every day*

  "I AM Creativity"

  "I AM Honor"

  "I AM Flow"

  "I AM Feelings"

  "I AM a Miracle"

  "I AM Spontaneous"

  "I AM Abundance"

  "I AM Safe"

  "I AM Harmony"

  "I AM Life"

  "I ALLOW myself to FEEL"

  "I AM a Creative Being of Light and Love"

  "I HONOR my Sacred Body"

"I AM Open and Receptive"

"My Sexuality is Sacred"

"I AM letting go of Anger"

"I AM Letting Go of Control"

"I AM Letting Go of Judgement"

"I AM Flowing with Life"

3. Solar Plexus Chakra (Sanskrit name: Manipura)

The *Solar Plexus* Chakra is situated at the upper part of your belly, right above your Sacral Chakra, and underneath your rib cage. It expands into your diaphragm, upper abdominals, stomach, pancreas, spleen, liver, gallbladder, and all throughout the digestive system. The Sanskrit name for this Chakra is *"Manipura"*, which is translated into *'Shining Gem.'*

This Chakra is all about *"Self-Mastery"* – the ability to master your thoughts and emotions, overcome any fear, and take appropriate action in any situation. This Chakra is the center of self-assertion, dynamism, and confidence. This Chakra's energy raises our bar for risk-taking and enhances our critical thinking, as well as our logical reasoning. Our willpower and the strength of our commitments are also greatly affected by the third or Solar Plexus Chakra. It defines us as a person. All our habits and desires, which descend from our subconscious mind, sit here. They provide us with a sense of individuality and self-independence.

Affirmation - Mantra

"I Can," "I Do."

Fire provides vitality and sustenance to all living organisms on our planet and is the element of this Chakra. On a physical level, Manipura focuses on our digestion system's vital processes and metabolism. It is also our psychic center, controlling and providing the instinctive drive to find vitality, self-empowerment, strength, morality, integrity, action, and individuality. It is the center of our personal *"Will and Power."*

The *'Sun'* represents this Chakra, as it radiates vitality and energy, providing it to every living creature on Earth. Since the stomach is the source of energy for our body, it is also the center point of our body's *"Life Force Energy."*

Overactive and Underactive Third Chakra

The *overactive* stage is recognized by the flow of personal power from our life into the lives of the people around us. Anger, greed, over-ambition, and a lack of empathy are common symptoms of this case. Physical effects such as digestive problems and imbalances in the pancreas, appendix, kidneys, and liver can also occur.

The *under-active* stage fuels insecurity and compromises self-esteem. It usually occurs when our personal power lies in another's hands or when we are in a helpless situation. We may feel incredibly needy and timid at times and flushed with indecisiveness. When this energy center is closed, we may experience digestive disorders and other malfunctions, such as ulcers, gallstones, hypoglycemia, and/or diabetes.

Healthy and Balanced Third Chakra

If your Solar Plexus is balanced, you will feel full vitality, with an enhanced ability to take responsibilities. Your self-discipline gets drastically increased. You will become more spontaneous, reliable, more risk-taking, confident, empathic, warm, and playful – someone who truly enjoys life.

Conclusion

- **Location:** Upper abdomen, stomach.
- **Corresponding gland:** Pancreas.
- **Focus:** Self-worth, self-esteem, emotional intelligence.
- **Color:** bright- electric yellow.
- **Sense:** Vision, will, and power.
- **Element:** Fire.
- **Verb:** "I can," "I do."
- **Age of development:** Between the ages of 15-21.
- **Demons of this Chakra:** Strong and excessive ego, shame, low self-esteem.

Practice

- *Focus your attention towards your Third Chakra, upper abdomen.*
- *Imagine a bright yellow, spinning tornado coming out from the front and back of your Third Chakra' physical body, expanding outward into your aura.*
- *Affirm 3 to 5 times every day:*

  "I AM Confident"

  "I AM Reliable"

  "I AM Spontaneous"

  "I AM Powerful"

  "I use my Power wisely"

  "I AM Unique"

  "I AM Light"

  "I AM Divine"

  "I AM Discipline"

  "I AM Commitment"

  "I AM Authentic"

  "I AM Myself"

  "I AM Honor"

"I Take Action"

"I HAVE Boundaries"

"I AM Empowering Myself"

"I AM Honoring My Individuality"

"I AM Responsible"

"I AM Taking Responsibility of my actions"

"I AM Shining My Light"

"I AM practicing Self-discipline"

"I AM Letting Go of My Ego"

"I AM Co-creating with God and the Universe"

4. Heart Chakra (Sanskrit name: Anahata)

This Chakra is situated behind the sternum at the center of your chest and level with your heart organ. It is associated with the heart, lungs, circulatory and respiratory systems. It is considered the bridge between the lower and the upper Chakras. It influences our ability to give and receive love from others, as well as the ability to love ourselves. The Sanskrit name for this Chakra is *"Anahata,"* which means **'unstuck or unhurt.'**

Affirmation - Mantra

"I love," "I give," "I receive," "I forgive."

The element of the Anahata Chakra is **'Air.'** This Chakra is directly related to our *breath*. On a physical level, the Anahata Chakra relates to areas that include our upper back, chest, arms, fingers, heart, lungs, breasts, thymus gland, circulatory system, and respiratory system. The Heart Chakra represents our ability to love ourselves unconditionally. It provides the ability to give love to others as well as to receive love from others. Additionally, you will be able to trust yourself as well as trust other people and the universe, become more grateful, and have the capacity to forgive – while also being compassionate, kind, and empathic.

Overactive and Underactive Fourth Chakra

Overactivity of the Heart Chakra can lead to obscure personal boundaries. We start building toxic relationships with ourselves and with others. We make these unhealthy choices, all in the name of love. We may find ourselves prioritizing other's needs before our own. This can present itself as an attachment, overflowing emotions, manipulative tendencies, overbearing care-taking behavior, excessive social validation, narcissism, and egotism. This over-activity can also adversely affect our health, which includes increased heart rate, heartburn, palpitations, and unhealthy interpersonal skills in relationships.

On the other hand, the **under-activity** of the Heart Chakra usually results in fear of rejection and being hurt. We feel that it's better to create a protecting wall around our hearts and never really grow close to anyone. This will eventually make us feel out of place and lose our sense of belonging. A sense of belonging is a human necessity, just like the need for food and shelter. To feel that we belong is very important and essential for the good functioning of our Heart Chakra. This chakra's under-activity could also be manifested in our life in the form of health problems like asthma, high blood pressure, heart disease, lung disease, and/or other respiratory issues.

Healthy and Balanced Fourth Chakra

If your heart chakra is in good health and balance, you will be able to accept, respect, and love yourself unconditionally, as well as others. You will be caring, compassionate, empathic, peaceful, kind, and have a sense of contentment coming from within. You will have the capacity to give and receive. You will be able to forgive and be compassionate to yourself, as well as towards others.

Conclusion

- **Location areas:** Heart, lungs, breasts, thymus gland, circulatory system, respiratory system, chest, upper back, arms, hands, and fingers.
- **Corresponding gland:** Thymus.
- **Focus:** Love, joy, forgiveness, compassion, harmony, relationship, gratitude, mind-body connection, and spiritual growth.
- **Element:** Air.
- **Color:** Bright – electric emerald green and/or pink.
- **Sense:** Touch.
- **Verb:** "I love," "I give," "I receive," "I forgive."
- **Age of development:** Between the ages of 21-28.
- **Demons of this Chakra:** Grief and Hate.

Practice

- *Focus your attention towards your Fourth Chakra, at the center of your chest.*
- *Imagine a bright, emerald- green spinning tornado coming out from the front and back of your Fourth Chakra's physical body – expanding outward into your aura.*
- *Affirm 3 to 5 times every day.*

"I AM Love"

"I AM Lovable"

"I AM Giving Love"

"I AM Receiving Love"

"I AM Kind"

"I AM Joy"

"I AM Content"

"I AM Acceptance"

"I AM Grateful"

"I AM Compassionate"

"I AM Peace"

"I AM Harmonious"

"I AM Forgiveness"

"I AM Light"

"I AM Life"

"It is only when we silence the blaring sounds of our daily existence that we can finally hear the whispers of truth that life reveals to us, as it stands knocking on the doorsteps of our hearts."

–K.T. Jong.

5. Throat Chakra (Sanskrit name: Vissudha)

The ***Throat Chakra*** is located inside your neck, around the throat region. This Chakra governs your throat, cervical areas, thyroid, and parathyroid glands, esophagus, larynx, neck muscles, shoulders, auditory system, and vocal cords. All of which are related to communicating with ourselves and with others. The Sanskrit name for the Throat Chakra is ***"Vissudha,"*** which means **'*To Purify.*'** We may speak with our tongue, and our voice may come from the throat, but the **'*truth*'** comes from the fifth Chakra.

Affirmation – Mantra

"I Speak," "I Listen," "I Express."

This Chakra helps us speak the truth and let us see the truth within us and around us. This truth also helps us determine what we truly want. It amalgamates all our creative energies and channels toward something productive. Vissudha Chakra is also responsible for providing us with the ability to listen to others, as well as to be heard by others.

At the Throat Chakra, there are two types of Extrasensory Perception (ESP) present, *Telepathy and Clairaudience.* These are senses we all have, and with ample meditation, we can awaken and develop them.

Telepathy is a gift that we all possess, and telepathic abilities are much more natural than one might think. Telepathy is the process of receiving another person's feelings, emotions or thoughts. Telepathy usually happens over distance and without the use of other senses like hearing or touch. Like a radio, every one of us contains the ability to transmit many frequencies – the same principle on which telepathy works. When we can align our frequency with the vibration of another person, we can communicate telepathically.

Clairaudience is the other Extrasensory Perception (ESP) ability that we can awaken. Clairaudience is having a capability of receiving an intuitive vocal message from the world of spirits or a higher being. People who are Clairaudient can extend the "range" of their hearing far beyond our regular, physical world and our known level of awareness and reach to much further extents. Clairaudients are highly intuitive people who can listen to a voice other than their own when the spirit world transmits a message to them.

This Chakra represents a spectrum of inner senses we communicate. The element of this Chakra is *'Sound'* and is related to our *voice*, to speak the truth, self-expression, vibration, creativity, inspiration, sound, music, authenticity, honesty, verbal, and non-verbal communication.

Overactive and Underactive Fifth Chakra

A person with an *overactive* Throat Chakra will be someone that interrupts others without caring for their feelings or opinions —a person who tends to be critical, bossy, and over-opinionated. Someone with an overactive throat Chakra will most likely be verbally abusive and raise their voice and interrupt people due to the need to be heard. People with an overactive Throat Chakra will also show poor listening skills. The physical manifestation of an overactive Throat Chakra could appear as mouth and jaw problems, grinding teeth, chronic sore throat, colds, earaches, neck pain, laryngitis, and/or thyroid problems.

When *under-active,* you will experience the inability to speak your truth, express yourself freely. You might be misinterpreted or misunderstood by others. You will be afraid to openly express your views, stand up for yourself, and express your feelings. Your self-esteem will diminish, and feelings of insecurity, nervousness, and anxiety will fester. If the energy of our Throat Chakra is blocked, we also might experience thyroid problems, hearing problems, sore throat, stiff neck, colds, and sinus infections.

Healthy and Balanced Fifth Chakra

If your Throat Chakra is in good health and balance, you will be able to express yourself in a healthy, honest, and kind manner. You will be creative, helpful, and will be able to ask for help when you need it – without hesitation. You will have the ability to express yourself, people will listen to you, and you will have the ability to listen to others.

Conclusion

- **Location:** Throat, cervical-spine, thyroid gland and parathyroid gland, esophagus, larynx, neck, shoulders, and all the auditory system.
- **Corresponding Gland:** Thyroid.
- **Focus:** Self-expression, truth, creativity, inspiration, and communication.
- **Color:** Bright – electric Cobalt blue and /or turquoise.
- **Sense:** Hearing, sound (auditory).
- **Verb:** "I express," "I speak," "I listen."
- **Element:** Akasha, Ether.
- **Age of developments:** Between the ages of 29-35.
- **Demons of this Chakra:** Lies, secrets, and ignoring the truth.
- **Extra sensorial Perceptions (ESP):** Telepathy and Clairaudience.

Practice

- *Focus your attention towards your Fifth Chakra, your Throat.*
- *Imagine a bright, turquoise color-spinning tornado coming out from the front and back of your throat, expanding outward into your aura.*
- *Affirm 3 to 5 times every day.*

"I AM Truth"

"I AM Communication"

"I AM Voice"

"I AM Creativity"

"I AM Clarity"

"I Am Honest"

"I Am Faith"

"I AM Integrity"

"I AM Healthy"

"I AM Joy"

"I AM a Good Listener"

"I AM a Good Communicator"

"I AM Expressing myself creatively"

6. Third-Eye Chakra (Sanskrit name: Ajna)

The *Third-Eye* **Chakra** is located between the eyebrows, over and behind your eyes, in the center of your head. The Sanskrit name for this Chakra is *"Ajna,"* which means '*to perceive and to command.*'

The Ajna Chakra is the center of intuition and foresight. The principle of openness and imagination drives the function of the Third Eye Chakra. This Chakra is responsible for developing and awakening your *Clairvoyant* ability. (ESP) – Extra-Sensorial Perception.

The Ajna Chakra is associated with the element of *'thought.'* The third eye illuminates everything as it is, without the filter of our past, beliefs, expectations, or judgment. This Chakra provides insight or vision that transcends the physical and material world. It is the Chakra of *time* in where time is timeless. This Chakra allows us to perceive the concepts between life and death through wisdom and truth.

Affirmation – Mantra

"I See," "I Trust," "I Believe."

The Third-Eye or Ajna Chakra represents the connection or bridge between the physical – material world and the metaphysical world. Working with this Chakra allows us to use our third eye to access cosmic visions. This Chakra is our visualization center for imagination and insight. When we open it, we start experiencing intuitive dreams, insights, and symbols that guide us through life, just like a map. This is where our psychic abilities, psychic perception, clairvoyance, and intuitive knowledge are born and developed. This Chakra is associated with the metaphysical aspect of how the universe works and what it is made of. It allows us to see the truth and helps us cultivate trust in one's own intuition and insight.

Overactive and Underactive Sixth Chakra

The *overactive* state of the Third Eye Chakra can have drastic effects on our psychological behavior, like finding ourselves fantasizing, hallucinating, feeling anxious, and constantly overthinking, resulting in mental drain and delusions. Some physical symptoms also could appear, which include headaches, insomnia, nausea, and loss of memory.

When **under-active,** you might feel stuck in your rational, analytical mind and ignore your intuition. You will be afraid of the unknown and be indecisive, confused, with a lack of direction and purpose in life. You will feel the inability to let go of the past, and your fear of the future will increase. You might also experience mental cloudiness, stress, depression, anxiety, allergies, sinus infections, and a failure to retain information.

Most likely, a person with an under-active Ajna Chakra may fall prey to illusions and be more easily manipulated. The Third Eye Chakra is the spiritual center, which interacts with the rational mind to deepen our intuitive insight to see beyond the veil of illusion. Opening the mind and discriminating between thoughts motivated and strengthen by fear and illusion are all challenges of the sixth Chakra. The key here is to learn and develop an impersonal mind by detaching yourself from physical and mental illusions. In doing so, you can transcend your thoughts, worries, and fears and truly know your soul from within.

Healthy and Balanced Third Eye Chakra

If you have a healthy and balance Third Eye Chakra, you will develop a strong intuitive sense. You will become creative. This creativeness will also spill over to your subconscious, allowing you to recall dreams much more clearly. This will help provide a more guiding vision for life. You will notice an overall improvement in your memory, and the heightened creativity will allow you to visualize better. For developing a healthy and balanced Ajna Chakra, it is essential to stay grounded. The Third Eye Chakra teaches us to see the truth and instills a unique sense of spiritual discernment and awareness within us.

Conclusion

- **Location:** Between the eyebrows, over and behind your eyes in the center of your head.

- **Corresponding Gland:** Pineal.
- **Focus:** Imagination, wisdom, intuition, insight.
- **Color:** Bright – electric Indigo, green or purple.
- **Verb:** "I see," "I Trust," "I Believe."
- **Element:** Thought.
- **Age of developments:** Between the ages of 36-42.
- **Demons of this Chakra:** Lies, secrets, illusions.
- **Extra Sensorial Perception (ESP):** Clairvoyant.

Practice

- *Focus your attention towards your Sixth Chakra, between your eyebrows, in the center of your head.*
- *Imagine a bright indigo/green-colored spinning tornado coming out from the center of your head front and back and expanding outward into your aura.*
- *Affirm 3 to 5 times every day:*

    "I AM Vision"

    "I AM Healthy"

    "I AM Awareness"

    "I AM Discernment"

    "I AM Intuition"

    "I Believe"

HEIDI MORRISON TEACHINGS

"I AM Insight"

"I AM Truth"

"I AM Intelligent"

"I AM Bless"

"I AM Open"

"I AM Wisdom"

"I AM Trusting Myself"

"I SEE the Truth"

"I Believe in Myself"

"I Believe I deserve all good live have to offer"

7. Crown Chakra (Sanskrit name: Sahasrara)

The Crown Chakra is situated right above our head in the center. It is mainly related to the pituitary gland and secondarily with the hypothalamus and pineal gland. The two glands work in pairs to maintain the endocrine system. Due to the placement and location of this Chakra, it is associated with the nervous system and the brain. The Sanskrit name for this Chakra is **"Sahasrara,"** which means **'One Thousand Petals Lotus.'** This Chakra connects us with the universe and the Divine source of creation. Sahasrara defines your state of consciousness and is considered as the gateway to meet the divine self. The energy associated with Crown Chakra unravels the mystery of the universe through harmony and oneness.

Affirmation – Mantra

"I Know"

The Crown Chakra helps us to let go of pride and ego and allows us to move beyond selfishness and other confinements. Sahasrara Chakra is a **'cosmic consciousness'** that exists within us. It is an element of oneness and thought, with everyone and everything. It is founded by a pure sense of transcendence.

The Crown Chakra represents the ability to live in the present moment, the here and the now, our connection to the source. Spiritual truth, divine wisdom, enlightenment, and a feeling of oneness with the Universal Consciousness all derive from this Chakra.

Overactive and underactive Seven Chakra

When this Chakra is *overactive,* the ego might increase negatively, making the person proud and selfish. It is the place where most likely, this person will use their power unwisely, just for the benefit of the Self. On the other hand, if this Chakra is *under-active,* this person is least likely to experience any spiritual connection and feel lonely and disconnected.

Healthy and Balanced Seven Chakra

If your Crown Chakra is healthy and balanced, you will attain the highest level of consciousness and enlightenment. You will feel joyful and peaceful. You will feel connected to the universe. You will give to the universe without expecting anything in return. You envision everything and everyone as equal and united.

Conclusion

- **Location:** Top of the head.

- **Corresponding gland:** Pituitary.
- **Focus:** Spiritual connection, divine wisdom, enlightenment, oneness, universal consciousness.
- **Color:** Bright White, purple and/or rainbow.
- **Sense:** Empathy, unity, oneness.
- **Verb - Mantra:** "I Know."
- **Element:** Divine consciousness, thought, oneness.
- **Demon of this Chakra:** Pride.
- **Age of development:** Between the ages of 43-49.
- **Extra Sensorial Perception:** Clair-cognizance.

Practice

- *Focus your attention towards your Seventh Chakra, your Crown, at the top of your head.*
- *Imagine a bright, purple-colored spinning tornado coming out from the top of your physical head and expanding outwards into your aura.*
- *Affirm 3 to 5 times every day.*

   "I AM Knowingness"

   "I AM Awareness"

   "I AM Divine"

   "I AM Humble"

"I AM Empathic"

"I AM Purity"

"I AM Unconditional Love"

"I AM Consciousness"

"I AM Unity"

"I AM Oneness"

"I AM Communion"

"I AM Peace"

"I AM Expansion"

"I AM Inspiration"

"I AM Understanding"

"I AM Wisdom"

"I AM ONE"

"I AM Surrounding to the Divine within and without"

"I AM Universally Aware of all Beings"

Our Energetic Anatomy forms the basis of who we are at the core of our being. Our subconscious and conscious mind is connected with the energy field that not only surrounds us, but permeates around our body. This includes all our memories, imprints, emotions, desires, believes, and habits.

All physical, mental, and emotional disorders can be perceived as disharmony in our energy fields. This **'disharmony or dis-ease'** indicates that we have gone out of tune – our vibrational rate is out of balance, and/or our body has lost its rhythm. In other words, if any of the Chakras spins too much, too little, or gets blocked, our health will inadvertently get affected. The Chakras in our body can be aptly compared to the floors of a building. These specifically designated areas in our body take in information from the outside world, process it inside ourselves, and express it outwardly in various forms. Therefore, chakras can be called the centers of energy, the places where life pro-creates and gives us a safe space to express ourselves.

By tuning and balancing our bioenergetic anatomy (Chakras and Aura), we can diminish and even resolve the disharmony in our being. By assisting and helping these systems in our body, as they get stimulated, our body begins to heal itself, right down to a cellular level.

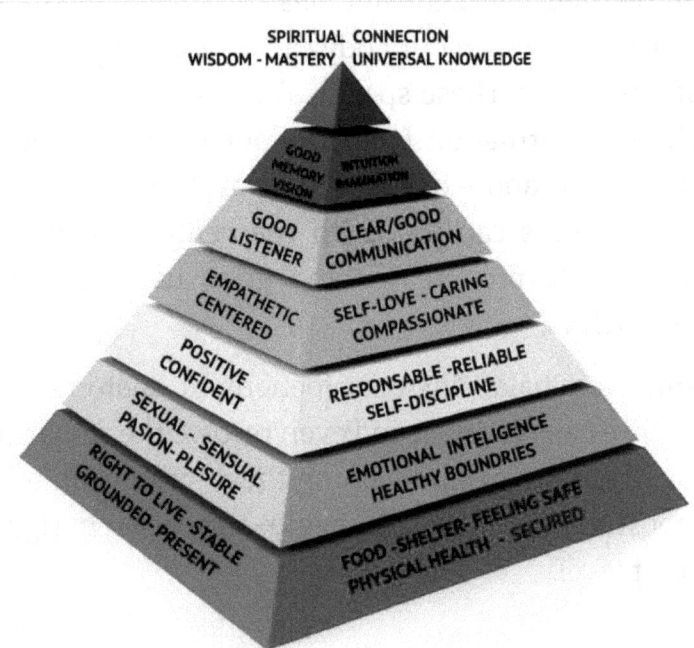

The 7 Chakra System Pyramid

Chapter 8: Consciousness

"The movement of creation and action in life is the root substance of consciousness of your 'I AM' Self, meaning the individual who is awake and aware to his source of creation and perfection of life, expressing himself thru all Divine characteristics and qualities of Love, Wisdom and Power."

–Heidi M. Morrison.

The "I AM" Presence"

Your **"I AM Presence"** is the essence of God and the **'Seed of Consciousness.'** The consciousness of God's Son, Jesus Christ, is centered in this flame, thus called the Holy Christ flame. Your heart is the place where God's flame – your **"I AM"** gets ignited the day you incarnate.

God's sacred fire's trinity has all the qualities of **'Power,' 'Wisdom,'** and **'Love;'** every quality needed to make your **"Ascension."** The flame in your heart is the **'seat of cosmic consciousness,'** and it is what links your soul to your divinity and your potential for Godhood.

"Only after becoming self – conscious can we open the doors of universal consciousness"

–Debasish Mridha.

The "Three-Fold Flame"

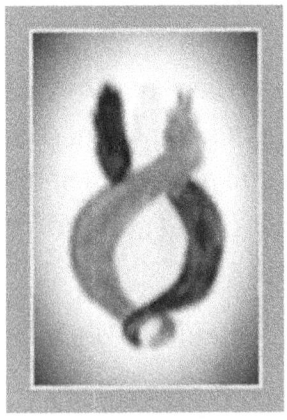

The *"Three-Fold Flame"* is located inside of your heart. It is composed of three inter-related flames, which are blue, yellow, and pink in color. The colors represent the energies of *The Father (blue), The Son (yellow),* and *The Holy Spirit (pink).* It is also where our Body, Mind, and Soul integrates. It represents the trinity of *Divine Wisdom, Divine Power, and Divine Love.*

The Blue Flame

The blue flame represents the flame of *Divine Power,* which manifests as our inner drive and resolves to accomplish the soul's desires to work in alignment with God's Will. It is a proper representation of the great innate leadership qualities present in you, as well as proper, balanced use of the *Will and the Power of God.*

The flame of the Divine Power empowers us to have goodwill and faith, allowing us to achieve our purpose and completing tasks. To find the strength to accomplish *'Mind over Matter'* is achieved here. Apart from our psychological strength, the blue flame also relates to our physical strength and stamina of our bodies. People with a tall blue flame tend to have more physical energy and have more *mechanical intelligence.*

The Yellow Flame

The Yellow Flame represents the flame of *Divine Wisdom*. It manifests as our cognitive abilities; to learn, understand, process information, and reach self-realization – a state of illumination. It helps guide us to use the right things at the right time, use the right words with the correct information, and just be at the right place at the right time. It also helps us be fair, unbiased – genuinely neutral. This can only begin manifesting when you truly ponder inwards into your own being. Discover your own truths, which ultimately will help you discover a whole new world of information inside of you. This is the place where your sense of knowingness gets seeded and starts growing.

The yellow flame directly correlates to your cognitive thinking within your auric field. People with a tall **yellow flame** tend to be very intellectual and are intelligent in the traditional way – *mentally*.

This flame teaches us the correct use of the knowledge of all *Universal Truth*. It gives us the inner urge to be a source of wisdom and knowledge and preach what one has learned to better others' lives.

The Pink Flame

The flame of *Divine Love* manifests as our ability to feel and express unconditional and compassionate love, the very nature of God. This is the kind of love that differentiates between empathy and sympathy. It is empowering and liberating – not limiting or controlling.

People with a tall pink flame tend to have much more compassionate energy, are more understanding, and have a very keen sense of *emotional intelligence.*

Ascension

As you start to gain mastery in the soul plane by nurturing, balancing, and expanding your *"Three-Fold Flame,"* you will start to experience the full communion with Ascendant Masters, Angelic Presences, and Celestial/Light Beings that will be available to assist you in fulfilling your life's purpose on Earth.

The process of *"Ascension"* is the act of rising into a higher level of consciousness. The self-liberation and realization process of Ascension depends on how much the individual allows and opens themselves up to its idea and invests its energy into that direction.

Ascension is the reunion of the soul with the spirit of the living God, the *"I AM Presence."* This happens when we humans have balanced our Karma and have bought our divine plans (Dharma) to fulfillment.

The first step in this involves merging into the Christ Consciousness, followed by the reunion with the living presence of your *"I AM THAT I AM."*

Ascension is a monumental moment in the life of a person. The Soul (the corruptible aspect of being) becomes a permanent atom in the body of God. It attains the status of the *"Incorruptible one,"* – which frees the person from the complications of Karma and the cycle of rebirth. Ascension is ultimately the process of accepting and allowing yourself to become *"ONE"* with your Creator, enabling you to receive all the blessings your Creator has in store for you. The Ascension process has no discrepancy – it does not exclude anyone on any basis, neither caste, creed, nor religion.

"Our Creator is all about Unconditional Love, Compassion, Unity, Understanding, Forgiveness, and Joy. He is waiting with open arms for every one of us to come back home."

-Heidi M. Morrison.

When we nurture the qualities of self-love, compassion, kindness, understanding and forgiveness in our hearts, we move closer to becoming *One* within ourselves, and ultimately with our Creator.

It is essential to know that our Creator does not punish us – we are the ones punishing ourselves. *How is that possible?* We do that by separating ourselves and living in duality within ourselves and with others, thus, with our Creator.

For any soul to walk on the *'Path of Ascension,'* it is crucial for them to balance their Karma and fulfill their Dharma. This *'Path'* is a way of life – the ultimate goal that one aims to achieve.

By working on ourselves, making a conscious effort to be mindful, our consciousness begins to rise. All the innate qualities inside us and our God's -Self starts flourishing. Feelings of love, kindness, compassion, and understanding start to develop inside ourselves, becoming Peace and Joy the forefronts of our life.

The shift of consciousness that our mind goes through, is the answer to our evolution. When we keep ourselves open to spiritual growth, all of the qualities that are not yet aligned with the Christ Consciousness begin to align themselves. These precious Christ qualities add wholeness to our lives. It provides us the vision to live life whole-heartedly, in communion and unity within ourselves and the entire Universe.

Christ Consciousness

The energy center of *"Christ Consciousness"* is located above our crown, in our etheric body - on our **8th Chakra.** Christ Consciousness is the highest consciousness that knows that **ALL** of us, even the smallest living cell, is a seed of the Higher Divine Intelligence that we call God – our Creator.

Christ's Consciousness reminds us of the *"Law of One."* It is the One connection and inter-relation within and without. It is the spark of life projected from our *'I AM Presence'* through our *'Christ – Self'* for the purpose of our soul's evolution.

Practice:

- *Repeat these affirmations – mantras, for at least 3 times every day.*

    "I AM Christ Consciousness"

    "I AM the Universe"

    "I AM This"

    "I AM That"

    "I AM Everything"

    "I Am Water"

    "I AM Earth"

    "I Am Air"

    "I AM Fire"

    "I AM Sound"

    "I AM Vibration"

    "I AM Awareness"

    "I AM Consciousness"

    "I AM ONE "

Our Christ Self is the mediator between God and Us. We can only experience Christ Consciousness when we accept and integrate our true nature – *'We are a Soul in a body, having a human experience. Death is an inevitable part of life. Our physical body dies, but our Soul is Eternal.'*

The Soul is Eternal and goes on to Ascend to what we know as the *'Higher Self.'* Our mind is interconnected to God's mind, into the Christ consciousness mind. By getting to know yourself, cultivating a more profound and honest relationship within, you open yourself to the cultivation of a more in-depth and direct relationship with God. Once we accept and integrate our true nature, our Body, Mind, and Soul become **ONE**, within and without.

Jesus Christ teaches us to:

"Open our Hearts to LOVE - to Ourselves and Others,"

"Live in COMMUNION- with Ourselves and Others"

"Live in UNITY - with Ourselves and Others"

"TO DO ALL things, from a Place of LOVE"

To love ourselves and others, is to love God. To live in communion and unity with ourselves and others is to live in communion and unity with God, our Creator. In the eyes of God, we are **ALL equal.** There is no difference between individuals of different races, religions, beliefs, or social/economic classes.

The Soul Star – 8th Chakra

The *'Soul Star Chakra'* is the eighth Chakra and is located above our Crown Chakra. This is the place where we experience a profound *"union"* with the entirety of creation and with our Creator. It exists in our energy field and hovers above our heads like a star. We often see this Chakra's illustrations in paintings, as a radiant halo above the head, most notably surrounding Jesus Christ, Mother Mary, Buddha, and other spiritual figures.

This Chakra is unaffected by the death of the body; it acts as a template to *'create '*our physical body. The attribute of the eight Chakra is invisibility. In this center, we become **The Observer** and **The Witness.** It is that place where we experience new heights in the level of awareness. This includes all of the things and even the events around us, which we experience through our senses. It is the place where we **'*Become*'** who we truly are – at our soul level.

This Chakra serves as a connection and a gateway to the furthest reaches of the Universe and the *'All that there is.'* It is our direct connection to our *'Higher Self.'* Due to the fact, the Soul Star is the point of our transformation, it is sometimes considered as *'the origin or seed of design and creation'* of the seven lower Chakras, which relate to us as an incarnated entity.

Overactive and Underactive Soul Star Chakra

Just like all the other Chakras, the Soul Star Chakra has states of over-activity and under-activity as well. The signs of an *overactive* Soul Star Chakra are similar to those of an overactive

Crown Chakra. A person might feel ungrounded, disassociated from Earth, confused, light-headed, and with a lack of purpose. The physical manifestation of an overactive Soul Star Chakra could be in the form of constant headaches and dizziness.

On the other hand, an **under-active** Soul Star Chakra can manifest itself as moving in life without a direction, and as a consequence, a lack of ability to find purpose in life. Emotionally, this can manifest as depression, cynicism and anxiety. A person may not be able to establish faith and trust, spiritually and ultimately, in themselves.

Conclusion

- **Location:** Above the crown chakra.
- **Color:** Gold.
- **Focus:** Design and create the incarnate body.
- **Sense:** Transcendence and timeless.
- **Element:** The Soul.

Practice

- *Repeat these affirmations 3 to 5 times every day.*

    "I AM a Miracle"

    "I AM Universal Truth"

    "I AM Universal Love"

"I AM Universal Wisdom"

"I AM Whole"

"I AM Unity"

"I AM Communion"

"I AM Ascension"

"I AM Light"

The Seat of the Soul – 9th Chakra

The 9th *Chakra* is known as the *'Seat of the Soul.'* It is located outside of our energy field, extending throughout the universe and far beyond time and space. It is always *crystalline* and *pure* and is the place where we can experience the magnificent expansion of creation.

The 9th Chakra is the place of *'Becoming,'* associated with the Eagle's perpetual state – which brings in vision, clarity, and foresight. The *'Eagle'* represents the fourth level of perception. It teaches us to soar above the highest valleys but still be able to see the trees, rocks, and rivers below. Eagles are known for their keen vision, being able to see objects from miles away. Whenever storm clouds gather, they get excited as the Eagle uses the storm's wind to lift itself higher, far above the clouds, to see things other birds simply cannot. Eagles can see the big picture – while also keeping all the small details in focus. The Eagle's great wings hold the heart, which teaches us to see with the *'Eyes of the Heart.'*

The Eagle allows us to rise above the day-to-day life struggles that occupy our lives and consume our energy and attention. The Eagle provides us with the wings to soar above the trivial, unimportant events into the high peaks of Heaven. In Eagle, the reality is perhaps about 99% consciousness and 1% matter. The brain associates with this level of consciousness correspond to the prefrontal cortex, which some neuroscientists call the *"God-brain."*

At the 9th Chakra, we no longer perceive ourselves as disconnected from the planet or other people. Instead, the boundaries we have set up seem to melt away as our individual Soul recognizes our Oneness.

Conclusion
- **Location:** Above the 8th chakras and outside your energy field.
- **Element:** Spirit.
- **Color:** Crystalline, pure light.
- **Sense:** Liberation, freedom, oneness, empty space.

Practice:
- Repeat these affirmations 3 to 5 times every day.

  "I AM Timeless"

  "I AM Space"

"I AM Free"

"I AM Purity"

"I AM Creation"

"I Am Magnificent"

"I AM Expansion"

"I AM Consciousness"

"I AM Vision"

"I AM Clarity"

"I AM Perception"

"I AM Infinite"

"I AM Crystalline"

"I AM Divine"

"The act of observing alters the reality of being observed."

–Heisenberg Principle.

Chapter 9: Forgiveness

"Forgiveness is a divine quality that transmutes all negative patterns and dissolves Karma. It acts as a doorway to Self-liberation, Self-realization, and Ascension."

-Heidi M. Morrison.

Forgiveness is the compassionate feeling that supports a willingness to forgive and show mercy. The main components that define forgiveness are two fundamental ideologies,

1. To stop being angry,
2. To stop being angry about.

"We must develop and maintain the capacity to forgive. He who is devoid of the power to forgive, is devoid of the power to love. There is some good in the worst of us, and some evil in the best of us. When we discover this, we are less prone to hate our enemies."

-Martin Luther King, Jr.

When we forgive, we allow ourselves to restore and renew our oneness with our Christ Self and liberate ourselves from all forms of self-limiting believes and ideas that bound us to the self and to others.

Forgiveness is the highest expression of Love. It comes from deep within your heart, a place of peace and unity. As we allow this energy to flow through us, only then will we be able to expand it all around us.

It is important to remember that without forgiveness, we cannot make any spiritual progress. Every time we forgive, we move one step forward into becoming *'One'* with our *"I AM Presence."* On the other hand, every time we hurt someone and upset them, we move one step back and separate ourselves from God.

As we grow spiritually and learn to unconditionally love ourselves, the process of forgiveness becomes more effortless. By becoming a *'neutral observer,'* you will learn that people who are causing you pain are just suffering themselves. As you are able to see the truth in that, you will begin to develop feelings of compassion, understanding and love that will allow you to forgive and love yourself and others.

When we don't forgive the people who have wronged us, either with an unfair, unjust, unfaithful, or un-loyal action, we tie ourselves to them with *Karmic chains*. These *Karmic chains* are reinforced by our negative thinking, words, emotions, and actions. All of which originate from a place of resentment, anger, sadness, hatred, and guilt either toward our own selves, or towards others. As these negative emotions increase, they become poison to our bodies, blocking energy flow in our energetic and physical anatomy.

> *"Anger is an acid that can do more harm to the vessel in which it is stored than to anything which it is poured."*
>
> -Mark Twain.

By allowing yourself to *let go* of the story, detaching from it, it becomes much easier to begin the forgiveness process and stop the Karmic Chain from building up. These chains are reflected in us physically, as emotional anguish. You will keep repeating the same story over and over again, continuously thinking and fantasizing about the past. You might find yourself asking, *why? what if?* You may end up blaming the other person or even yourself for the outcome. Can you see these negative emotions how they keep you from living in the present, unable to enjoy life? Can you see how much these emotions drain your energy and ultimately affect your health?

On the other hand, think about the feeling of love, understanding, compassion and forgiveness. These positive energies will *charge* you with even more energy, infusing you with **Life Force Energy** – full of happiness and good health. *Be curious! Explore your feelings. Observe, and discover how you feel.*

> "Darkness cannot drive out darkness; only LIGHT can do that. Hate cannot drive out hate; only LOVE can do that."
>
> *–Martin Luther King, Jr.*

The Ego

That part of us that doesn't allow us to let go and forgive is our **'Ego Self'** or **'Lower Self.'** It is that part of you that has been hurt and doesn't know how to love because it has never been loved. Forgiveness doesn't begin by having an outward look at our personalities and forgiving those who have hurt us. It begins inside of us. To forgive yourself' is one of the most important things you must remember and practice. Ironically, it happens to be one of the most indispensable things to accomplish as well. To forgive is to allow yourself to let go of the events that have happened and to accept it as it is. To forgive is to learn from our mistakes and live life in the present moment. When we don't forgive, we are continuously dwelling in the past. Every time someone hurts you, emotionally, mentally or even physically, it wounds you. Charging this wound with resentment solves nothing; it only makes things worse for everyone and creates *Karma*. The energy of the *'eye for an eye'* mentality keeps the vibrations of a person very low. Let go of the anger and resentment inside you, allow the **"Laws of Grace"** to intercede, and dissolve the Karma you have stored in your Akasha.

"An eye for an eye only ends up making the whole world blind."

- Mahatma Gandhi.

Forgiveness is a choice. We cannot control other people's actions or reactions, but we can control our own actions and reactions. This means you are primarily responsible for your own happiness, peace of mind, and ultimately your liberation. When we're looking for forgiveness from someone, what we're really seeking, is the other person's acceptance, acknowledgment, and most often, love. Forgiveness is about offering all these things to ourselves first, which brings us freedom. By working on forgiving ourselves and everyone who has put us in emotional and even physical turmoil, we liberate ourselves and others.

The most challenging part of the Ascension Process is to understand the meaning of forgiveness. When we point fingers at people, blame others, or even at ourselves, worry excessively and near-constantly – arguing about our pain and suffering, we are keeping ourselves trapped in the lower vibrations of duality and non-love. Learning to forgive helps us experience Unconditional Love, liberating us of all burdens.

"If every human being recognized the power of love and forgiveness principle, all consciousness on Earth would change instantly."

-Kuan Yin.

Practice

- *Make a list of all people you have ever hurt, as well as a list of people who have ever hurt you, intentionally or unintentionally.*
- *Start by putting your attention into your Heart Chakra, breathing in a soft Pink Light of Unconditional Love, Acceptance, and Forgiveness.*
- *As you breathe out, expand the soft pink light into every cell of your body., as well your whole aura – creating a pink bubble of light all inside and around you.*
- *Feel the emotions of unconditional love and forgiveness.*

- *Once you embody this light and emotions, call into the Angels of Forgiveness and Unconditional Love to surround you, as you imagine them all around you – at the edge of your Aura.*
- *Invite and welcome the first person on your list into your circle, see them coming towards you as you imagine them in your mind's eyes.*
- *Now, open your heart to forgive and ask for forgiveness.*
- *As you forgive, imagine a karmic cord getting detach from your energetic body.*
- *As you let go, imagine the cord dissolving and disappearing.*
- **Affirm 3 times**

> "I Forgive you (<u>name of the person</u>) and Let Go.
>
> **Thank You, I Love You!**"

- *As you let go of the first person, invite, and welcome the second person on your list into your circle of unconditional Love, Forgiveness and Acceptance – and continue until you finish your whole list.*

Often, it takes more than one time to ask for forgiveness or forgive the other. Be patient, compassionate, and understand yourself, the other, and the situation.

> "Forgiveness is the remedy for the pain caused by you, to yourself, and to others. It's the highest level of human intelligence."
>
> —Heidi M. Morrison.

Letter – Asking for Forgiveness

Dear <u>(name of the person who you are asking forgiveness from)</u>,

I'm here asking you for forgiveness. If I have ever caused you pain of any kind, intentionally or unintentionally, in this incarnation or other incarnations, please forgive me, and liberate me from all attachments and Karmic cords.

Thank you, I love you!

<u>(Your signature.)</u>

Letter – To Forgive

Dear <u>(person's name you want to forgive)</u>,

I forgive you for all pain you have cause to me intentionally or unintentionally, in this incarnation or in other incarnations. I forgive you, and I am liberating you from all attachments and Karmic cords.

Thank you, I love you!

<u>(Your signature.)</u>

Forgiveness Decree – Prayer

"I AM Forgiveness within,

I AM Forgiveness without.

I AM forgiving myself,

I AM Forgiving You.

By the Law of Grace,

I AM Asking for forgiveness today.

I Love and Forgive myself,

I love and Forgive you all."

(Repeat 3 times)

Affirmation

"I AM now letting go to all fears, attachments, influences and frequencies, from my physical, mental, spiritual and emotional bodies that are not serving me for my highest good and greatest joy."

"I AM now welcoming all experiences that filled me with Joy and are aligned for the highest good of everyone connected to us."

(Repeat 3 times)

"Forgiveness comes from deep inside your Heart. It is unconditional love in action and the highest expression of Love."

–*Heidi M. Morrison.*

Chapter 10: Judgment

"Those who are highly evolved maintain an undiscriminating perception. Seeing everything, labeling nothing, they maintain their awareness of the Great Oneness. Thus, they are supported by it."

-Lao Tzu.

The universal spirit does not judge us. We humans have created judgments to compare, contrast, control, and define labels as good or bad, right or wrong, beautiful or ugly. We judge ourselves and others against artificial and often idealistic standards of perfection, morality, and /or truth.

Every day, we are surrounded by judgments, whether on tv, social media, in our mind, feelings, actions, and even in the way we express ourselves. Without us realizing it, judgment has the ability to alter our own mind, feelings, actions, and even the way we express. The society we live in has been doing this for a long time now; categorizing, labeling, and comparing everything, and everyone, making this judgmental behavior prevalent – making people believe this is okay. It is essential to understand that just because this is a prevalent behavior doesn't make it *'beneficial'* for anyone. It certainly harms all of us by creating more separation with everyone around us, as well as within ourselves.

Let's understand why people judge themselves and others. **"Mr. and Mrs. Judgement"** is *[Your Name] Judgement Self* – just another version of you that needs acknowledgment, attention, love, and the need to be understood. This part of you is like a little child that is acting up because it wants to be noticed; it feels scared and left out and needs attention.

Your *"[Your Name] Judgement Self"* is neither good nor bad; we shouldn't judge it. Just like when a good friend of yours is going through a hard time. The best and perhaps the most immediate remedy for them is to welcome them with an open heart and a warm hug, to be listened to, and just be with - without judgment. This part of you, needs exactly the same.

The Principle of Correspondence

"As Within, So Without, As Above, So Below"

-Hermes Trismegistus.

For every physical phenomenon, there is a corresponding mental and spiritual phenomenon. It assists us in seeing that which our physical eye cannot, through our perceptions in life.

"As Within, So Without, As Above, So Below." Embody the truth that there is always a correspondence between all the planes of existence as everything comes from *'The All,'* and everything exists according to all laws of creation. The thoughts and images we hold in our conscious and subconscious mind manifest themselves in a near mirror likeliness of our external circumstances.

> What we think within ourselves will be reflected in our external physical world; in other words, what we put out is what we will get back.

As above – as in Heaven, our own mind,

So below – as on Earth, our physical body/environment.

If we think positive, pleasant experiences will reflect back to us; if we think negative, unpleasant experiences will reflect back to us. Your physical reality is a holographic reflection of what you firmly believe to be true. Just like a mirror, reality is subject to change with the reflection. Therefore, our judgments attract judgment to us in equal measure. Planet Earth is a *"School"* for practicing these laws and experiencing life.

Our *'perception'* of things is unique to us. We see things through the eyes of our own experiences, our history, our values, our preferences, our beliefs, and our biases.

Each person has a unique *'personality spectrum'* or *'lens'* that reveals how they see the world and experience life. As we learn and grow, our personality spectrum or lens changes. In the process of change, we often have a hard time communicating with those who have a different perspective. This is because all paradigms around us are influential. For this reason, it is important to open our minds and agree to disagree. Each person's view is unique, and everyone has the right to have their view respected by others.

I have also observed and experienced that most people repeatedly ask me the same question, *'Is that good or bad?'* I always have the same answer: There is no good or bad. What really is good or bad? What can be good for me, can be bad for someone else and vice versa. A more appropriate question to ask to ourselves or to others would be,

'Is it beneficial for ...?'

I really like the word *beneficial* because it has a positive connotation as it includes more than one person. **Beneficial** here means favorable, helpful, constructive, benign. It indicates-

"For the highest good of everyone connected to."

It is a generous, helpful, kind, humanitarian, useful, gratifying, healthy, big-hearted, and favorable word. Like we learned before, words carry energy, and it is vital we do our best to utilize this energy wisely.

"Carefully watch your thoughts, for they become your words. Manage and watch your words, for they will become your actions. Consider and discern your actions, for they have become your habits. Acknowledge and watch your habits, for they shall become your values. Understand and embrace your values, for they become your destiny."

–Mahatma Gandhi.

Practice

- *Start by observing your "[Your Name] Judgment Self" from a neutral perspective.*

- *As you start breathing in and out into your heart chakra, (at the center of your chest), open your heart widely, and welcome that part of you that has been hurt or ignored.*
- *Acknowledge that part of you that has been rejected now for a long time. Listen to him/her and be with it - without judgment.*
- *Say **"Hello"** and welcome them with an open, warm, and loving hug.*
- *Tell them:*

  "I See You, I Feel You, I Know You, I Love You!

  Forgive me for ignoring and judging you.

  I will not abandon you again."
- *Most important, listen to what they have to say - give it time - **BE** with it - without rushing it - or judging it.*

It is essential that you don't ignore or reject that part of you, as that will only result in an increase of feelings of insecurity, fear, sadness, anger, guilt, shame, and even resentment.

We can also observe that some people like to judge or bully others because they have a misleading belief that it's a way to assert dominance, – to have power and control. The truth is, that people behave like that because they feel very insecure, weak, and not in control. There are also situations where many people express hurtful opinions to others, coming from a place of non-love. They may call this *joking around,* but in reality, it is bullying. We must recognize the fact that there's a very fine line between *joking* and *bullying* - the effects of which are equally damaging.

"Judging is a way of intellectual bullying. No one has the right to hurt you, nor you to hurt others. Judge not today!"

–Heidi M. Morrison.

All of us know how it feels to be judged by someone else; it wounds us. That wound may intensify with time, and sometimes it may even be carried over lifetimes. Intentionally, hurting another person not only damages the person in different ways, but it also creates separation between the two, with the Self, and consequently, creates **"*Karma.*"**

In today's society, we can observe that humanity acts and reacts mostly on an **'*autopilot.*'** How many times have we woken up in the morning, looked at ourselves in the mirror, saying, *'Oh, my! I look terrible /fat /ugly /old,' and so on,* beating ourselves up. Does that sound familiar? Believe it or not, that's self-judgment. In essence, you are bullying your own self, which results in non-self-acceptance and love.

"Pay attention to the thoughts and words you express to yourself, as there is not a worse enemy than your own Self."

–Heidi M. Morrison.

This unconscious behavior leads to polarization and separation from our true Self as well as the entire world around us. This is what we refer to as our Yin/Yang polarity not integrated, and it is what divides and anger not only our own selves, but also large and small communities all around the world. It is important to understand, recognize and accept our differences (nor good or bad), be able to assess similarities, and know that no one is better or worse than anyone else, just as no one is better or worse than you.

In the previous chapters, we discussed how our thoughts, words, and actions carry vibrations and how these vibrations help shape our reality. It is time we start updating our minds with newer, loving, and beneficial software. By using the power of awareness, you can access all your sub-conscious, unconscious, and prevalent behavior. As you begin to pay more attention to your thoughts, feelings, actions, and reactions, you will be able to stop yourself and change them to aid you constructively.

Learning to Discern

To discern, is to have the ability to comprehend the smallest details accurately, while maintaining the ability to simultaneously understand their differences. This allows intelligent judgments to be made due to this process. *Discernment* may seem like judgment, but there is a significant difference between these two approaches for life. The word discern comes from the Latin dis- off, or away + cernere – to distinguish, shift or set apart. Hence, to discern means to differentiate and or "sort out" what is considered from God, what is considered as "flesh" and even what is considered from the devil. Discernment is a conscious approach that is personalized according to each individual. It's that person's cognitive ability to distinguish between right and wrong. With discernment, we make beneficial choices for ourselves and for others. To discern is to have the ability to see into something from our *Higher Self perspective,* not from our Lower-Self, rigid standards, opinions, or societal pressures. It's that place where we can transcend our ego to see the truth, using the ability to perceive clearly.

> *"Discernment comes from understanding – to have a neutral, clear and detach perception of what really is and isn't."*
>
> *–Heidi M. Morrison.*

The inner essence of all things is the spirit itself. Divine energy constitutes the true nature of existence. Therefore, judgment doesn't serve us in meditation, but discernment can. To quieten down our minds, we need to discern between what's real and what's not.

Practice

- *Make a conscious decision **not to Judge** today. Instead, learn to **discern**.*
- *Become the Eagle inside you and observe the whole picture – without judgment and from a **neutral perspective.***
- *Start with 5 minutes a day.*
- *Be curious, see what life teaches you, stay positive, aware, and Have Fun!*

"Happy people are frequently discerning and improving themselves. Unhappy people are mostly criticizing, disapproving, and judging themselves, and others."

–Heidi M. Morrison.

Chapter 11: Intentions

"Life is a creative series of actions; we are always creating whether we know it or not. The key is to stay aware of this fact and use it to our advantage."

-Heidi M. Morrison.

An intention is a mental state that embodies an agreement to carry out an action or a result. This involves mental activities such as forethought and planning. It determines any idea that is planned or has the intention of being carried out. Your goal, purpose, or aim is your intention. It is the creative power that fulfills all our needs, whether they be in our physical, mental, emotional, or spiritual aspects of life.

All intentions begin with a single thought; thoughts have immense power. They are a subtle nuance with an immense, vital, and irresistible force that is ever-present in the Universe. Our mind can assume the form of anything it contemplates. You can even try this out right now. Try thinking about any object and you can visualize it in your mind.

"If our thoughts change, so will our reality."

-Heidi M. Morrison.

Intentions are a direct impulse of consciousness. It contains the *seed* from which we *create.* Just like an actual seed, intentions cannot grow if you hold on to them. They will only come to fruition when you release your intentions into the fertile depths of your consciousness and then nurture them.

Dr. Masaru Emoto – a water researcher and Japanese scientist, is known to have studied the fascinating world of water and how vibrations and sounds can infiltrate deep enough to affect the molecular structure of our human anatomy, as well as our planet.

"The Power of Thought"
(Water experiment)

Dr. Masaru Emoto spent years studying **water crystals** by employing High-speed Photography and Magnetic Resonance Imaging (MRI). This device uses powerful magnets, radio waves, and a computer to make detailed pictures. He used these devices to measure the energetic vibration and rhythm, testing the water to record human beings' emotional and vibrational patterns. His years of research had concluded that water does indeed react profoundly to sounds and vibrations.

Water crystals seem to take different forms depending on how they were treated, and the kind of thoughts and words were spoken to them. Beautiful geometric shapes with bright colors resulted from kind and loving words, like *'Thank you'* and *'I Love you,'* whereas negative, harsh thoughts and words crushed the crystals forming destructed and asymmetrical shapes will dull colors. This experiment was directly linked to human consciousness and how we human beings result from our thoughts, and the words we speak, and the words spoken to us.

Whatever we input into our systems gets translated and sent out as output. The fact that our human body and our planet are made approximately of 70% to 75% water, our thoughts and words have a profound repercussion on our health, well-being, and on our home Planet Earth.

"Every thought, every word is impressed upon it and carried out in amazing detail. It is like a singer making a record on the sensitive disc of the photographic plate. Every note and tone of the singer's voice is registered. If he coughs or hesitates, it is also registered. So, let us break all the old bad records in the subconscious mind, the records of our lives which we do not wish to keep, and make new and beautiful ones."

-Florence Scovel Shinn.

The Law of Intention

The *"Law of Intention"* states that what happens to us in life is created not by what we do, but by *"why"* we are doing it.

Integrity

'*Integrity*' is the quality of being honest and having strong moral principles, while also maintaining those standards consistent throughout every part of the Self. Integrity is the state of being complete, undivided, undamaged, and uncorrupted. When we are integral, we speak from a place of wholeness. Our words match our intentions, thoughts, and actions. When we break from this pattern, utter sentences which hold no truth and are not a reflection of ourselves, we move out of integrity.

Suppose someone does something with some ulterior motive or to be in a position of advantage, power, and control (over someone, something, or some situation). In that case, that person is not acting with integrity and will not be destined for higher rewards *(bad Karma)*. All efforts and intentions must attain a higher vibration to reach a higher spiritual accomplishment level and be rewarded for the good deed *(good Karma)*.

> *"Say what you mean and mean what you say."*
>
> –Dr. Seuss.

Thoughts have the power to create or destroy; they are a creative, dynamic force. By shifting them in a positive direction, they work miracles. If you can hold positive thoughts (high-vibrations), you will be able to enjoy a pleasant and healthy life. On the other hand, by holding on to the negative thoughts (low-vibrations) in your mind, you will eventually create disharmony in your life.

The Principle of Mentalism

"The All is Mind; The Universe is Mental."

-Hermes Trismegistus.

The Mental Universe can be described as a space with an intelligence field and is infinite. The foundation of everything, physical or spiritual, is mental in nature. All the signs of life, energy, and matter that we experience on planet Earth are figments of the infinite living mind's thoughts. It puts consciousness over matter and energy. The principle of mental substance applies to all planes, for all are held in the mind of **'The All'**.

Every *thought* has its own mental image that is impressed upon our subconscious mind and carried out in detail. Every person's mental image is different. Their views, sentiments, feelings, habits, experiences, and ways of thinking are all different. Every *action* has a past that lead to it, and a future that follows it. Each *thought* we have is a sort of connection to an endless cause and effect; in where each thought become a cause, and each cause has an effect.

Practice

At the end of every day, reflect on your day by asking yourself. Today,

- *Have I brought happiness, solutions, and light into my life and other people's life?*

- *Have I brought chaos, drama, and darkness into my life and other people's life?*
- *What can I do to better myself and others?*
- *What can I do to better my life and the life of others?*

Repeat these affirmations 3 to 5 times every day:

"I Am Aware of my thoughts, and

I Am using them wisely,"

"I Am Aware of my intentions, and

I Am using them wisely,"

"I Am Aware of my words, and

I Am using them wisely,"

"I think, I feel, I speak, and I act with full integrity.

For everything I Say, and I Do, to be for

The Highest Good of Everyone Connected to Us."

"Everything is Energy, and that is all there is to it. Match the frequency of the reality you want, and you cannot help but get that reality. It can be no other way. This is not philosophy. This is physics."

- Albert Einstein.

Chapter 12: Let go

"We cannot sail our ship when the anchor is holding it down. We need to pull the anchor up, so our sail can catch the winds and move us ahead."

–Heidi M. Morrison.

'Letting go' means being willing to allow life to take you to a new place, a new direction. It is the activity of freeing yourself from painful memories, thoughts, unhealthy habits, possessions, and even toxic relationships with other people, as well as with your Self.

Letting go also applies to stop worrying about the past and the future. We human beings are very interesting and hilarious at the same time. We live life thinking that when we are worried, it's a way we care, and when we don't worry, we worried because we don't have any worries. It is time to know the truth.

Vibrationally, the feeling of worry is destructive, low, and negative energy, just like fear, anger, shame, guilt, hate, and jealousy. Every time we worry about something or someone, we are attracting more of this kind of energy into ourselves and sending this lower - negative energy to the person or situation we think we are helping or care that we care about. **Worrying** is not an emotion that brings any kind of benefit to any solution. The more we worry, the more worry we attract, and as a consequence, things get worse.

Here is when many other universal laws and principles play their role. *Letting go* might seem difficult to do, but as you learn about how all universal principles and laws work, it becomes possible with some training and practice.

"The law of Non-Resistance" teaches us that whenever we resist any situation, we provide more power to it – making the problem increasingly difficult to solve.

"What you resist always persists."

-Carl Jung.

This is because whenever you resist something, you direct more energy toward that object, making it stronger. Therefore, it affects you more negatively. Sometimes, the problem may seem too big – you might think it's unsolvable! This causes feelings of disempowerment and would make anyone lose hope. The first sign of resisting any situation is when you begin to struggle with it. Every time you struggle, you are going against the flow. Change the direction whenever you notice that you are struggling.

"The best way to approach any problem is to acknowledge it first. Observe the given situation from a neutral perspective, which allows you to assess the situation for what it truly is."

-Heidi M. Morrison.

Positive energy is infinite; whenever you give out positive energy, you receive it in return. Whenever you take a positive action to solve a problem, you will receive a solved problem in return. By choosing to take a positive direction rather than the negative one, you make the law of non-resistance work in your favor. If, for any reason, you can't seem to figure out a way to solve a problem, leave it. When you come back to it at a later time or date, you will notice that the problem was solved by someone else or, you might discover a new way of solving it. This only becomes a possibility if you leave the situation as it is – with a peaceful mind rather than worrying about it all day.

Going with The Flow

We've all heard this phrase, but now, let's understand it with a more holistic view. *'Going with the Flow'* is all about releasing resistance and letting go of all thoughts, people, and situations that cause us emotional discomfort. In essence, it's to *'turn your boat downstream'* without resisting the current of the stream and allowing it to take its course. Whenever we think we can't solve a problem we face in our lives, we are going against the flow of life and not with it. In other words, we are going *'upstream.'*

> *"By flowing in life, we move toward our life Purpose."*
>
> *–Heidi M. Morrison.*

On the other hand, whenever we feel like life is going our way, everything is going great, and we either solve problems ourselves, or someone does it for us; we might be assuming that we're lucky, but there is no luck. It is the simple fact that we are finally going with the flow, utilizing the law of non-resistance to our benefit, and identifying the correct path intended for us to continue our journey, allowing ourselves to start moving forward again. Similarly, the people who consider themselves unlucky when things don't go their way, is because they are just going in the wrong direction.

Whenever you are faced with adversity in your life, do not resist it. Instead, acknowledge it, surrender to it, and learn to take action from the present moment and a neutral perspective. By doing that, the direction you will take will always be the best one.

At its core, resistance is fear – fear of the unknown, fear of the simple fact that we cannot. This *fear* arises from our unresolved issues – old vows and contracts made in this life and/or other lives and the Karma from our choices in those lives. Working with the *Akashic Records* is the best way to identify and let go of things that hold us back.

> *"Letting go is to surrender our ego and will, trusting in the Universe that whatever is necessary for our highest good and greatest joy will be provided to us."*
>
> *– Heidi M. Morrison.*

A lot of us need to let go of our conditioned thought patterns and belief systems. Naturally, this is a rather scary thing for a lot of us. To avoid our feelings, we process the same old, faulty belief system deep-seated in our minds until we are ready to make changes in our lives. In order to change these patterns, we need to release our negative thoughts and replace them with healthy, peaceful, and loving thoughts.

> *"To let go, is to allow energy to flow without controlling it. Step out of the hose and let the water flow."*
>
> –**Heidi M. Morrison.**

If we continuously find ourselves in situations that lead to unhappiness and frustration, it could be because we need to let go of the situation. This includes letting go of any and all drama in our lives. Certain changes in our life can put us on the path of betterment, changing jobs, moving houses, even changing friends and the way we interact with them. Sometimes, we are the ones that might be provoking the situation; in this case, letting go requires us to change the way we see things - to don't take things personally; to become the observer and contemplate the situation before making a decision.

Start by observing whatever situations would trigger your reactions. Whenever you catch yourself either blaming someone, or receiving guilt, blame, or shame, remind yourselves that you no longer wish to experience this in your life. **'Forgive yourself'** for interacting in this pattern, as well **'forgive the person'** who makes you feel that way. Once you think that you're ready to release this pattern, know that it was the time intended for you; this is the time where you have the opportunity to let go and grow.

Once you acknowledge the simple fact that something in your life isn't working, consider other possibilities. As you begin to ponder over your old patterns, you will discover new ways of living your life; you will learn to let go and trust.

> *"Letting go is a continuous process of changing and trusting. Forgive and Let Go."*
>
> *–Heidi M. Morrison.*

It is essential to remain present – at the here and the now moment. Continuously monitor your thoughts, feelings, and actions. Know that trust also serves us as a vital factor in letting go. Why? Because whenever we do let go, we move through the fear of the unknown.

Most people are afraid to let go because they are simply too attached to their worldly possessions, beliefs, habits, or the people they surround themselves with. When you're too attached to worldly belongings, you will find it difficult to let go of these harmful connections even when they cause you to suffer and leave you unhappy.

To experience a wider consciousness, a sense of freedom and happiness, we need to rise above our ego, soar like an Eagle and look at the whole picture. This is achievable by letting go of our thoughts, feelings, and memories that imprison us.

> *"Observe your thoughts, emotions, actions, and reactions. Recognize that whenever you experience a negative emotion, it is*

because of an attachment. Distinguish between the voice of the ego and the actual situation."

-Heidi M. Morrison.

By letting go of all our fears, moving into the present moment, centering ourselves in love and acceptance, we live in Divine Flow. It allows our higher self to flow through our lives. When we can achieve this, we will notice how we start to say just the right things – we do what's best for all of us and refrain from doing everything that either causes us harm or is non-beneficial for us — allowing us to maintain a stronger connection with our God-self.

Learning to be Flexible

Flexibility is the quality of being mentally and emotionally adaptable - open-minded. When we are flexible, we have acceptance toward everything, ourselves, those around us and the circumstances everyone is in – rather than have a rigid stance on things. To truly attain this, you need to have an alert and expansive state of awareness. You must also embrace things how they present themselves, utilizing your time constructively. A change in mindset also serves to be quintessential – problems are considered as opportunities for improvement, stumbling blocks become stepping-stones. Everything serves our highest good and greatest joy if and only we make good use of it.

The Serenity Prayer, drawn from Buddha's writings, used by Alcoholics Anonymous and various other twelve-step programs make good use of it:

"God, grant me the serenity to accept the things I cannot change, the courage to change the things I can, and the wisdom to know the difference."

Detaching from The Outcome

Detachment is the state of being objective and neutral. By exercising detachment, the letting go process becomes much easier. It will help you understand and recognize that every situation in life is an *opportunity* for self-growth and development. Even in cases where things don't work out the way we intend them to, if we observe all situations from a detached, neutral perspective, we will be able to see things clearly and have faith that they will work out in a beneficial way, trusting that a better opportunity will come our way.

"When we let go of all our expectations, we can change every aspect of life."

-Heidi M. Morrison.

Any habit of ours, beneficial or not beneficial, tends to restate itself over time. This will not stop unless we switch things around and break ourselves of that continuous pattern by engaging ourselves in something different. If it's beneficial, we can help reinforce this supportive pattern by using small, self-assuring rewards for ourselves. We possess the power of spontaneous action by doing our old hobbies or activities in new and exciting ways; the same applies for our life as we can change and restructure it, and ultimately our behavior. Our childhood plays an instrumental role in this as some of our abilities to alter and or change are dictated by what we were taught when we were young. We made sense of the world by observing patterns. We can correct non- beneficial habits by doing things differently, which will sufficiently interrupt the old pattern. *"The Law of Allowance"* recognizes that we all have choices; it brings freedom to our lives. It is the single-most fundamental law present in the Universe. The basic understanding of this law is that goodwill will only enter as long as we allow good into our life.

Emotions

Through emotions, we ultimately experience our reality. One way to view these emotions, are like *paintings*. Whenever we utilize positive emotions, our painting becomes more vibrant and colorful. Similarly, the opposite is true. Negative emotions paint our life with dark, dull colors.

Sometimes, we choose a positive emotion but don't allow positivity into our lives. This dis-allowance works as a negative paint, becoming neutral on our canvas. In a less metaphorical sense, this means that we not only need to put out positive emotions, but we also need to allow them into our lives as well.

To spiritually, surrender means to let go of everything that limits your soul to grow and no longer serves you. To surrender is to allow yourself to move without fear into the unknown, to welcome all infinite possibilities into your life, embracing your God-Self with Faith and Love.

"Be integral and clear on your intentions and allow goodwill to enter into your life."

-Heidi M. Morrison.

Chapter 13: Desire

"There is always plenty on man's pathway, but it can only be brought into manifestation through desire, faith, or the spoken word."

-Florence Scovel Shinn.

'Desire' is a powerful feeling of wishing, wanting, longing, or hoping for something to happen. Every action you intend to carry out begins with a thought, an intention that follows the desire. It motivates you to accomplish tasks and to work toward them. For example, if you desire to better yourself physically, you exercise and eat healthily, which in return will make you look better, move easier, and feel more confident. Similarly, if you want to get to know yourself deeper, you will meditate and practice mindfulness.

The bigger the desire, the greater the internal burning sensation you will feel inside you. The lower the desire, the less internal burning sensation you will feel, and eventually, it will fade away. It is important to focus your attention on this single question *'What do I want?'*

What Do I Want?

This is one of the most important questions we want to ask ourselves. It is a challenge and essential question that we honestly need to answer ourselves every day. There is also another aspect we must contemplate, and you've probably heard before, *"Be careful what you wish for."*

Awareness is absolute; in order to focus on our wishes or desires, we need to be aware of what we want. When we are unsure of what we want, we send mixed signals to the universe and the world around us.

I will teach you a secret on how to ask for what you want without the fear of the outcome.

Practice

- *Every day before you go to sleep, ask yourself - 'What do I want?'*
- *Write this question down on a piece of paper; if you know the answer, you can write it down.*
- *If you don't know what you want, don't answer it; just ask the question.*
- *Trust that the universe will provide you with the answer. The answer will come to you when you least expect it.*

What do I want?

"I want/ wish/ desire _____ [thing/ feeling/relationship] or Something Better, for the Highest Good of Everyone Connected to Us."

As a result, you will receive what the universe has in store for you without limiting yourself. Additionally, you do not create Karma with anyone – everything you want/wish/desire won't hurt you, as well anyone. Why? because it will be *"for the highest good of everyone connected to us."*

Remember, without awareness, you will never know when the answer is coming. Once you know what you want, the next step is for you to be very clear and specific about it. This is necessary because you don't want to send miss signals to the Universe.

In the process of finding what you want, you must also recognize and differentiate between your *'ego drive'* (things our ego needs) against your *'soul drive'* (what our soul wants). It does not matter how we will achieve it. By letting go and surrendering to the desire, we allow the universe to work for us. To be and stay positive and patient is key in this entire process. Sometimes, this process isn't as immediate as we would hope, but we need to comprehend why that happens. Understand that you are not alone in this world; other people also play a role in this existence, and they also have free will – just like you.

'Desire' takes determination, discipline, and commitment on the respective and appropriate *'Action.'* People with a strong, burning desire get results - they're the *'go-getters'* that don't stop till they get what they want. Keeping ourselves motivated is how a desire stays alive; it enables us to do big things. A low level of desire will further our relationships, our salary at work, or maintain a healthy body, bringing forth equally low results in our life. On the other hand, a powerful desire will always produce great results. We can achieve anything and everything that we desire only if we want to make it happen.

Think of desire like a fire; getting too close to a fire will burn you. If you can keep yourself detached from desire, you can nurture the fire - like adding wood to a campfire without burning yourself. Just like fire, desire is able to generate will, and put things in motion. It can start creating activities and accomplish them.

It is also necessary to respect desire - the same way you respect fire. If you want the flame to keep growing safely, you must pay attention to it. Fire creates and shapes things. You can use the element of Fire to transmute and transform energies. All our emotions, thoughts, and actions are like wood to feed the fire. Every action we take is moved by desire in some shape or form. It is the motivating power behind all our actions. We have the power to neutralize all the desires that aren't beneficial to us, as well as the power and free will to create new desires altogether.

Desire begins in the Mind, with the intention of the thought. It is vital to understand that whatever you desire won't always be manifested; for that reason, it is beneficial for you to put ONLY yourself in the picture, as everyone around you has *Free will* just like you.

The first step in the creation of Desire is formulating a concise yet important message of the multiple qualities and undertaking, as well as a complete, whole picture.

By visualizing Abundance, we can attract it into our lives – the same energy of success. This does not only imply money, but also abundance in relationships, health, spirituality, communication and so on.

> *"Energy follows thought; we move toward, but not beyond what we can imagine."*
>
> *–Dan Millman.*

Embracing Process

Achieving a goal is much more manageable if it's subdivided into smaller, incremental steps. Anything you would like to achieve, can be subdivided in easy and small to manage increments. Skipping steps or taking shortcuts often results in failure; we can't climb a ladder faster by skipping steps - most likely, and eventually, we trip and fall. It is important to appreciate and embrace the accomplishment of every step we take toward any specific goal.

> *"No matter what our innate talents are, it's only actions that will bring them to life."*
>
> *–Heidi M. Morrison.*

Chapter 14: Akashic Records

"The planetary etheric body is a whole, unbroken and continuous; of this etheric body, those of the healer and the patient are integral, intrinsic parts."

-Alice A. Bailey.

The word Akashic derives from the Sanskrit word *"Akasha,"* which means ether, atmosphere, or sky. In anthroposophy and theosophy, the *"Akashic Records"* are a collection of all universal events, words, emotions, thoughts, and intents that have ever occurred in the past, are currently occurring in the present or will occur in the future. It consists of everything's relations to every entity and life-form such as trees, plants, water, animals, the earth, and other living beings - not just us. The Akashic Records are encoded in a non-physical plane of existence, the **'Mental Plane.'** The Sanskrit term Akasha was introduced to the language of theosophy by H.P. Blavatsky, who referred to it as *"The Indestructible Tablets of the Astral Light."*

Akasha is the primary substance of the universe - a subtle, ethereal essence that fills the entirety of space. Akasha is the etheric energy that vibrates at a particular frequency to absorb and record every impression of life. Adepts can read these records with developed psychic faculties, as well, an ascended master or an un-ascended adept. They look at these records and can pinpoint any time or age since the Earth's creation and read the record of a specific time.

The Etheric Plane

This is the highest plane in the dimension of matter; it is concrete, real, just like the physical plane of existence, except for the fact that it is experienced purely through the senses of the Soul. This can be perceived with consciousness and beyond physical awareness.

On the Akashic plane, mankind's entire evolution registers collectively. The Akashic Records are an assortment of the entirety of knowledge present in the Universe – accessible through intuition, meditation, or astral traveling. Each of us is an essential component of the Akashic field, a worthy being holding a specific identity space.

This Universal Knowledge can influence our perception of reality and serve us as a tool of self-development. They are purely objective and unbiased. They do not pass judgments or label any action as *'good'* or *'bad.'* They simply record what has been, what is, and what will be. The Akashic Records are the epitome of wisdom and insight – revealing an individual's essence, expression, and potential. The Akashic Records have our soul's blueprints. It is an impression of our identity and our Soul's ultimate potential. These records offer guidance to clarify areas of our life, such as health, finances, career changes, relationships, and even inquiries about real estate, businesses, and pets.

Our destinies are never static. They are continually shifting due to our and everyone free will. When accessing the Akashic Records, it is essential to be clear on the information we are looking for, and what we plan to do with it. Another way to perceive it is to think of it as an infinite library with a nearly infinite number of books – even this is just a tiny drop of water in an enormous ocean. Keeping this in perspective, if you're looking for a certain type of information, you need to be specific. Like going up to a librarian and telling them the name of a book and author – you know what you want. Let's suppose you pick the wrong job; you don't like what you do. You can ask questions like, *"Why is this happening?" What am I supposed to learn from this situation?" "How can I change my perspective?"*

"The Akashic Records" are present in the Highest Dimension of universal knowledge; you must be in a state of openness, expansion, a high level of self-awareness, neutrality, unconditional love, non-judgment, and a non-ego state that is present in the here-and-now.

Accessing the Akashic Records

Accessing the Akashic Records can help us heal and grow by providing us the necessary understanding of events that will help progress our lives. When accessing the Akashic Records, we work with a team of spiritual beings, the *Lords of the Records - Masters and Spiritual Teachers*. In turn, they *'download'* the information you need and facilitate the process of opening the specific record that would be shared during that specific reading and healing.

The Masters and Spiritual Teachers

Your *Akashic Record Keeper'* will never tell you what to do. They simply reveal the information you are meant to receive that is for the highest good of everyone that is involved. The Masters and Spiritual Teachers offer direction and guidance to reveal the truth – always from a place of compassion, wisdom, and unconditional love.

They never expect anything from us, nor will they ask us for anything in return; they're simply omnipresent, offering their guidance by offering every possibility and probabilities from a higher point of view. As free-willed beings, we ultimately make the final decision. The Akashic Records offer everyone a new and open way of thinking, offering deep healing at the level of your soul. This is the part of your soul where you can access the spiritual perspective – the soul's point of view.

This is the highest form of Spiritual Counseling, offering guidance and insight with wisdom rooted in unconditional love for support, healing, empowerment, and transformation. The Akashic Records are not secret but Sacred. We must Respect and Honor them, only using them to:

"Serve the Highest Good of Everyone that it's Connected to"

To access our Akashic Records, we must transition from our ordinary state of consciousness into a Divine Universal Consciousness. It is the place where we recognize our oneness with the Divine at all levels. It is only in this state of consciousness that we are able to perceive the vibration of Akasha. When we access the records, we won't always hear what we want to hear. It is important to be open and to accept the information that we will hear.

In certain cases, this information can be uncomfortable, issues with unresolved Karma, past life experiences, and so on. Therefore, it is necessary to understand how this information can be utilized productively; with a certain degree of wisdom, it will help guide us into creating a more intentional life.

The very act of opening the Records can shift us to a higher energetic vibration. Why? because we're accessing Universal Wisdom in a conscious and powerful way. When we access the Akashic Records, we are asking for help, going beyond our comfort zone, and signaling to the universe, *"I'm ready to heal, please help me."* An Akashic reading goes beyond being just a reading – it is a form of *"Spiritual Healing."*

With an Akashic Record healing session, it is also a great way of identifying and canceling vows and contracts from your previous life. These vows engrave themselves on your DNA, your cellular structure, and your personal history (instinct). They recur throughout lifetimes unless you consciously and intentionally cancel them. The number of vows you could have made in your previous lifetimes could be numerous. These vows could include blocking creativity, shutting down your intuition, to cause self-punishment (through dissatisfaction jobs or toxic relationships). It also consists of helping everyone else before yourself (self-love), time limitation, self-esteem, financial limitations, eating disorders, drug abuse, and so on. All these vows are archived in your personal Records. Accessing this information allows you to gain consciousness of the contracts you've made. We can revoke them by using a specific protocol. From then onward, we can create new vows that will liberate you from the burdens of the old ones. The new contracts are much more freeing and expansive since they are made consciously and intentionally.

Chapter 15: Wisdom

"True wisdom comes to each of us when we realize how little we understand about life, ourselves, and the world around us."

- Socrates.

'Wisdom' is the quality of having experience, knowledge, and good judgment. It is the result of having the ability to discern what is true, right, or lasting, utilizing our own individual's awareness, knowledge, experience, understanding, common sense and insight. Wisdom is to look at the choices we make and the actions we commit from a higher perspective, like an Eagle, fly high and above the storm – to look at the big picture as well at every little detail inside of it.

"To be wise is to have the ability to examine, and consciously transform our intentions, thoughts, words, feelings, actions and reactions according to the highest good of all"

–Heidi M. Morrison.

One of our purposes as incarnated human beings is to acquire Wisdom. Knowledge without understanding whatever is learned will not make an individual wise.

True Wisdom is born from the understanding learned from personal experiences. It is to accept and love ourselves as a whole (light and shadow/yin and yang). It derives from utilizing our rational, logical abilities, together with our intuitive responses to comprehend the truth. This enables us to grow in awareness and then help us find our place and purpose within the universe, so we can lead a productive and fulfilling life.

To be wise is to have the ability to identify patterns that are harmful to us and break the cycle. Wisdom gained from experience last a lifetime. Take a class, learn, experience, explore, and be curious. Don't be afraid to make mistakes because they will teach you. To be wise is to know that we know nothing, and there is more in life. A wise person accepts everyone as it is, without judging them. To be wise is to be aware and to experience the wholeness of oneself.

Wisdom also represents a **paradox,** to accept and understand that we are wise and ignorant. A good person can be bad, and a bad person can be good. A wise person adjusts to these changes and let go of what is out of their control. A wise person lives life in the present and makes the best of every moment – good and bad, treating all of them as learning experiences.

Your Wisdom represents your truth, but it is only your understanding of the truth – your truth is not absolute. To be wise is to understand and accept that we don't know everything.

"We are all part of the Great Mystery of the Universe, limited by our own limited perception and understanding of what it is, was, or might be."

"Be Mindful,"

"Be Open"

"Be Curious"

"Be Aware"

"Be Present"

"The goal for having greater wisdom isn't to learn to use larger portions of your brain. It's about developing your intuition, your conscious connection, and your relationship with your Spirit part of you. As you flow this Energy of your Spirit Self more and follow your clear Guidance, you are accessing greater Wisdom in your life. Using your Intuition more is what then activates greater portions of your brain and gives you more Wisdom."

–Immanuel Kant.

Difference between Wisdom and Knowledge

Knowledge is everything you learn, either by experience or by education. Wisdom is the implementation of that knowledge in a way that benefits others. Knowledge is the awareness of what you know about a certain subject, thing, or even a person. It is the practical proficiency gained via education or experience. Simply implementing it is not enough. On the other hand, Wisdom is knowing when you can implement what you learned and where.

"Knowledge and understanding are the basis of Wisdom, but experience is key to attaining it."

-Heidi M. Morrison.

Wisdom unites Knowledge and Experience into insights and significantly increases a person's understanding of relationships and the meaning of Life itself. The nature of Knowledge is selective. Knowledge only stores specialized information, which because of its very nature, makes it restrictive. Whereas Wisdom is comprehensive and integrated. It has no limits! It can only provide positive results, since it is the implementation of knowledge with a benevolent attitude. Knowledge has a theoretical approach – Wisdom has a spiritual approach.

The Principle of Knowledge emphasizes the focused use of energy. As we can direct our energy and apply it to align ourselves to our goals towards the Highest Good. The more we hone our senses to this, the better we can tap into higher sources of Truth. Throughout our lives, we are introduced to a plethora of ideas and theories; by television, books, or from listening to other people's experiences. But, since none of that is from our own experience, it is not wisdom. Wisdom requires attention and a willingness to ask and to experience the truth. There is a noticeable difference when equates an experience from their personal lives or if it was just an idea. Ideas and knowledge are pleasing, but particular forms of truths must be tested in our hearts before they have any substantial power over our lives. You gain wisdom by investigating and testing the perspicacity of what is true in your life.

"Knowledge needs to be cultivated and then tested. Only then, will it mature into wisdom. "

-Heidi M. Morrison.

You should not believe something solely because someone told you, or it's written in a book. Believe it after you have tested it by yourself in your own heart and found it to be truthful and accurate. True *Wisdom* can only be attained by this type of inner-experimentation and willingness as well as an eagerness to experience.

"Knowing others is intelligence; knowing yourself is true wisdom."

-Lao-tzu.

Differentiating Truth

To discern between something that is true or not true is a question we human beings have had since the advent of civilization. When you repeatedly ask this question, you will find out that there isn't always a straight *'Yes – No'* answer to this. Instead, the question leads you to a deeper, more profound experience of it. The answer you derive from this is not just known intellectually, but **'known'** in your Heart and Body –

through your senses. Here is when *intuition* plays its role; ask the question and see where it takes you.

Intuition

To truly get in touch with our source of Wisdom and Intuition, we need to absolve ourselves from depending on others' opinions for our sense of identity and worth. We need to *trust* and *value* our own Intuition rather than give authority to other people's opinions over our internal feelings.

> *"Our natural intuitive powers become more profound when we acknowledge and follow our natural instincts."*
>
> *–Heidi Morrison.*

Once you understand how to put the knowledge you have learned in your life into beneficial practical use, only then, you will know, you have attained a certain level of wisdom.

Conclusion

"Life is a game with rules; there are billions of players that are interconnected – affecting one, affects everyone."

–Heidi M. Morrison.

Universal Spiritual laws are the rules, principles or patterns that can be applied to everything present in the entire Universe. It's important and very useful to be able to comprehend these universal laws as they serve as a guide to move around in life. Every human is born on this planet to experience life in a physical body. Being incarnated serves a simple purpose; to help us reach *'Spiritual Freedom'* and *'Enlightenment'* through the process of Ascension, which balances Karma through the mastery of our lessons.

Before our soul makes the decision to reincarnate, we create a *'blueprint.'* This is based on what our souls are the keenest to learn - to gain wisdom through experiences and knowledge for the growth of our Soul and Ascend. This blueprint includes elements such as our parents, siblings, gender, place and date of birth, the career(s) we pick, our financial status, our sexual preferences, our relationship(s), our marriage partner(s), children, and even the length of our life. We are also given 'free will' when we are making these decisions, which gives us the opportunity to learn through the use of our intuition and inner knowingness.

Lessons in our life can come from various situations, forms, life events, and people. How we respond to these elements determines whether we pass those lessons or not. Every challenge, obstacle, or negative experience present in our lives serves as an opportunity for us to learn and grow on a much deeper, Soul-level. Until we truly learn from these lessons, they will be continuously presented to us; manifesting themselves in different scenarios in our lives till we finally learn from them. The key here is to find the gift from the lessons presented to us and learn from them; that is how we regain our personal power, freedom, and wisdom.

As soon as we incarnate, we lose conscious awareness of our divine blueprints and the entire plan. As well as mapping out our blueprints before we incarnate, we also sign sacred contracts with spiritual guides to help and provide us with advice and guidance through our earthly journey. The spirit guide's main job is to guide us on our life's path and support us wherever we need it. Our spirit guide sends us messages via our subconscious mind. When we experience a synchronicity, our soul immensely resonates as it acknowledges the very blueprint – it's the moment when our soul recognizes that we're exactly doing what we're supposed to be doing. To be able to identify these events along our journey, we need to continuously remain aware and in tune with our intuition.

By understanding all these laws and principles, we can make use of them wisely, and master our own lives. We all have probably heard about the Law of Attraction. This is the primary law of all manifestation. To understand this further, imagine yourself as a magnet that is pulled toward whatever you're thinking or feeling. By doing so, if you feel fear, you cannot attract peace; if you feel anger, you will not attract love – and so on.

Every time we divert our attention and focus on anything, we call it towards ourselves. This is done with the help of our beliefs and our thoughts; - we invite experiences, situations, materials, and even people into our lives. They will arrive; if we don't want them, we drive them away.

As soon as you are ready to learn, the teacher will appear to provide you with that knowledge. This can be in multiple methods; a book, a TV show, a video on the internet, a person, a class – and so on.

Words such as *'don't,' 'can't,' 'won't,'* and *'not'* invoke resistance. This means that if you don't want to do, be, or have something, that is what exactly you will attract. For example, if you constantly think that you are ill, you will attract sickness into your life even if you're perfectly healthy. The opposite is also true – statements that reaffirm good health will bring that into your life. Saying, *'I welcome prosperity and happiness'* will bring that energy toward you.

Some people adopt a victimization mindset. They blame others for their fate and believe that the world owes them – wallowing in self-pity. Whenever someone thinks, *'poor me'* or *'I am so unlucky,'* they are cementing the victim mindset. People who blame others for their problems resist taking personal responsibility for what they have created themselves. Whenever we feel guilty or angry, we resist the joy of life.

The *mirror* of the Universe is flawless, accurate, and honest. Our inner-most desires are made evident in the reflections we see in ourselves. Every single person we interact with in life, acts as a mirror of an aspect of ourselves -whether it's negative or positive. Observe, identify, and see what the lesson is.

Whenever we feel as if someone else has the same emotions as us, it is a projection. We project the fears we have onto the world. Why? Because it's much easier to imagine someone else with the qualities we wish to deny within ourselves. On a more positive side, we also project our powerful, beautiful, and brilliant qualities onto one another. Every time you say or even think of something good/positive about the people around you, you act as a beacon that is projecting their internal qualities.

You can have practically anything you wish in your life. However, if your sense of self-worth depends on having it, then you have become attached to it. Anyone or anything you are attached to, holds the ability to control and manipulate you.

Karmic Chains are established between people who have unresolved situations between them coming from this incarnation or other incarnations. Every time you have thoughts and feelings of jealousy, anger, or hurt, you create a chain that attaches you to them. The same is true with objects. Having an expensive car, the latest cell phone model, an expensive house are all fantastic and beautiful things. But, if you need these things as a status symbol or provide you a sense of self-worth, it becomes a trap. Having attachments are a conditional form of love. Accepting someone for who they are is the true meaning of love.

An entire family can be tangled in cords of co-dependency. Feelings of guilt and shame bind people to memories, holding them back. The most effective way of dissolving Karmic chains is by Forgiveness. Our souls want us to face all our unresolved life lessons –and release them so we can move forward with our lives.

"Where your mind goes, energy flows"'

- Ernest Holmes.

Whatever you focus your energy toward, it will manifest. Spiritual laws ensure that an outcome manifests itself to the exact amount of attention you pay attention to. The only thing stopping you from manifesting your goals and desires are your own inner doubts and fears. Paying attention to negativity attracts it; paying attention to positivity attracts it. It takes a continuously prolonged negative mindset to bring negativity into our life.

However, just a minor positive influence quickly adds positivity to our life. How? Positive thoughts vibrate at a higher frequency; they move faster. In comparison, negative thoughts vibrate at a lower frequency, and as such, they move slower. Our Universe is the embodiment of energy; nothing is static.

The flow of Abundance is directed toward you. However, your thoughts, beliefs, self-worth, and memories create barriers to stop you from receiving them. It is your responsibility to break down these barriers and harness the flow of Abundance that is in your destiny. In essence, everything is about creating and maintaining relationships, starting from the relationship that you have within yourself.

To Love is being able to enjoy all your relationships. We block the Abundance that is destined for us when we close our hearts. The energetic vibration of Abundance is to learn how to *'give and receive.'*

The more we allow ourselves to receive from our own selves, the better we will feel. Once we are full of love, acceptance, and compassion, only then will we be able to genuinely nurture others. Being nurtured doesn't just stop at love and affection; nurturing means providing yourself with nourishing meals, a good night's sleep, exercise, meditation, positive and kind self-talk, etc. When there's a natural flow of nurturing emotion, we feel abundant and balanced in every way.

Remember: "We cannot love someone until we love ourselves first."

To be happier and fulfilled in your life, express it, and be grateful for everything. This, by itself, will make you feel happier and will direct the flow of happiness toward you. When you are clear about what you want, the Universe picks up on it. However, a lack of clarity blokes' psychic energy and keeps you in confusion. Attaining a sense of clarity allows you to move forward and provides you with more opportunities. Whenever you feel lost and frustrated without a clear sense of direction, wait patiently, the path will clear up for you, allowing you to make the correct move. Keep in mind; it's important to move, be it in any direction. So long as you move, irrespective of how difficult or cumbersome it may seem, only with clarity, can you open doors to the future.

Intentions followed by actions, are the force that makes things happen. Whenever Karma is assessed, the intentions - actions are taken into account. With honorable intentions and actions, we get rewarded — but only, if they benefit *'the highest good of everyone involved.'*

The act of *gratitude* can further assist you in this process. Energy flows in whenever you show an act of gratitude. Sending out heartfelt thanks for the blessings you have received only allows the divine energy of the Universe to lovingly respond to you by providing you with even more blessings. On the other hand, criticism and judgment are the opposites of appreciation and gratitude. Just as gratitude heals, judgment harms. Understand the fact that whatever challenges the Universe sends us, it is to help us grow. Our task is to appreciate and learn what we have been taught.

Along with appreciation, be graceful. Grace is something that we can offer and never run short of. By opening our hearts to receive Divine Love, compassion, mercy, empathy, and unconditional love, we can establish feelings of grace within ourselves. The more grace we offer, the more grace we receive.

We can only truly be grateful when we engage in prayer. Prayer is a form of tapping into God's power Source of energy. It benefits us greatly. On the contrary, worrying is the opposite of prayer. It is crucial to direct our thoughts in a positive, focused manner. Whatever you ask for in prayer, believe that you have received it. Faith is an important element that brings prayers to fruition. The very moment you begin thanking the Universe for its bounties, your faith will precipitate the arrival of your wishes; it automatically activates a response from the Universe. If, for example, you are praying for peace, feel the peace coming about, like on the shores of a beach. Prayer is always sincere and simple, always authentic, and from the heart.

Keep in mind whatever we experience in life will be in pairs. When we experience good, we will have to experience the bad. Our purpose is to integrate the natural polarities so we can live our lives in balance. This is subdivided into different forms of energy, such as masculine energy that provides us with aggressive, logical thinking, whereas feminine energy is more passive, creative, and intuitive. Find a balance of both of those types of energies while aligning yourself with positive and beneficial energies.

A lot of different aspects influence your Karma; your mindset is one of them. If you have a negative mindset, let's say you believe you 'aren't good enough,' this belief will ultimately become your reality by attracting this energy. Positive beliefs generate good Karma in your life, whereas negative beliefs do the opposite.

Remember, you are solely responsible for your own thinking patterns. Change your beliefs if they don't serve you in a positive-beneficial manner.

Every situation we encounter in life is due to the result of some kind of Karma we meant to balance. We continuously create Karma, both good and bad, from our everyday actions and even our intended actions, both consciously and unconsciously.

"Every thought, word, intention, action, non-action and re-action you have, affects your health, vitality, and ultimately your Karma balance sheet."

-Heidi M. Morrison.

The balance sheet of Karma is your *Akashic Records*. They are the culmination of everything about you and all your incarnations. The fundamental Law of Karma is, *"You reap what you sow."* In an effort to help resolve these internal conflicts, one can practice *meditation*. It helps us connect with our soul, alleviates suffering, and promotes healing.

Alongside meditation, *affirmations* are also something that can be implemented. By continuously repeating words/phrases, they can become a part of the subconscious mind and part of your internal *deprograming* and *re-programming*. Our subconscious/unconscious mind cannot discriminate and accepts all information as is. Therefore, whatever affirmations enter your subconscious mind profoundly affect how you feel, think and act. Everything from your emotions to your day-to-day activity is affected – ultimately affecting your life. You bring about what you affirm. '*Affirm what you want,*' and make sure your affirmation is purely positive.

A wonderful way to do this is by visualizing. *Visualization*, much like affirmation, is based upon the Law of Cause and Effect. Whatever you see or believe in, ultimately becomes a physical reality. Holding on to trust and faith forms a protective mold for your outer reality. We have the ability to create whatever we desire with our metaphysical powers. Whatever we focus on, it becomes a reality in our physical plane.

Manifestation requires Faith. Have Faith in yourself and the powers of the Universe. Another way to eliminate insecurities and establish a habit of self-love is by utilizing affirmations. Express what you desire, what you want, and repeat this consciously to the point your mind accepts them as fact. By adopting a positive perspective, we can change our negative thoughts to positive ones, ultimately attracting positivity into our life. Whatever your affirmation might be, make sure you put your heart and soul into it.[3]

Finally, if you have reached this point in the book, I would like to "thank you" for accompanying me on this wonderful journey.

I'm sure when you finish reading this book, you will get up with a change in your mindset and ultimately, a positive step towards improving your life!

---

[3] Visit my website www.heidimorrison.com for additional articles, services, and training.

*"The Universe is on your side, wanting to help you.
All you have to do is Ask and Allow yourself to receive."*

With lots of Love and Gratitude,
Heidi M. Morrison.

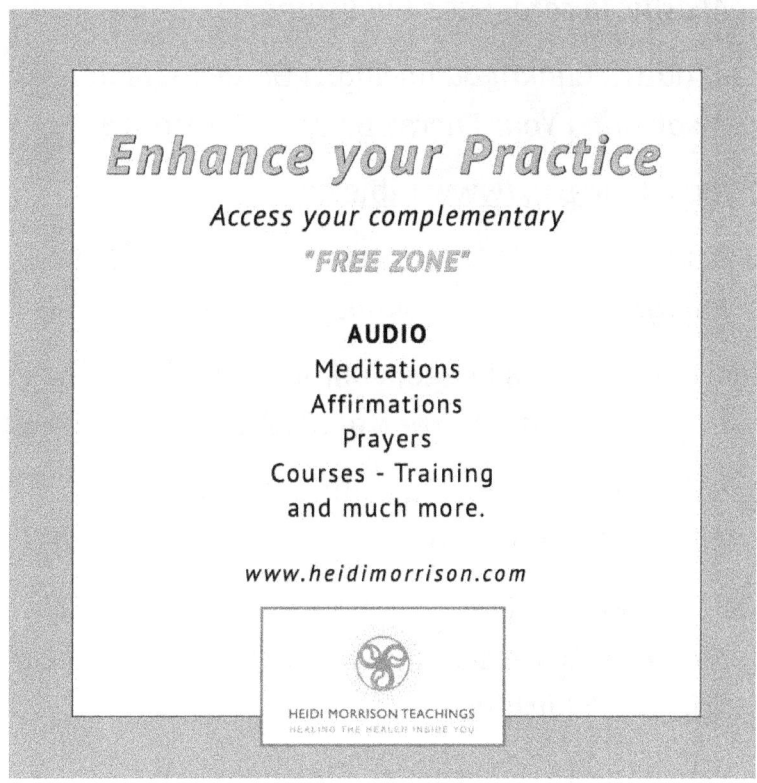

Bibliography

Alcoholics Anonymous, Serenity Prayer, extracted from Buddha's Writing, https://www.aa.org/

Alice A. Bailey, *Light of the Soul on the Yoga Sutras of Patanjali – Book 3: Union Achieved and its Results. Akashic Record*, Lucis Publishing Company, 1955

Andrea Judith, *Chakra Balancing: A Guide to Healing and Awakening Your Energy Body*, 1st Edition, 2004

Bible verses, https://www.bible.com/

Cindi Dale, *The Subtle Body: An Encyclopedia of Your Energetic Anatomy*, Sounds True, 2009

Confucius and James Legge, *Confucian Analects, The Great Learning & The Doctrine of the Mean*, 2016

Deepak Chopra, *The Seven Spiritual Laws of Success*, Amber Allen Publishing, 2015

Don Elkins, James Allen Mc Carty, Carla Ruekert, *The RA Material: An Ancient Astronaut speaks (Law of ONE)*, Schiffer Publishing, 1997

Dr. Masaru Emoto, *The Hidden Messages in Water*. Hillsboro, Ore.: Beyond Words Publishing 2004

Eckhart Tolle, *The Power of Now*, New World Library, 2004

Edgar Cayce, *The Akashic Records*, 1997

Eileen Day McKusick, *Tuning the Human Biofield*, 2014

Esther Hickes, Jerry Hicks, Wayne W. Dyer, *Ask and it is given: Learning to Manifest Your Desires (Law of Attraction Book 7) (Foreword)*, Hay House Inc., 2004

Godfrey Ray King, *Vol 2 - The Magic Presence (Saint-Germain Series)*, 2011

Goodreads, *https://www.goodreads.com/quotes*

Heidi M. Morrison, *www.heidimorrison.com* offers a comprehensive insight of everything discussed in this book. You can book sessions with me for a wide range of services.

Hermes Trismegistus, *The Emerald Tablets of Hermes*, Merchant Books 2013

Mark L. Prophet and Elizabeth Clare Prophet *Saint Germain on Alchemy: Formulas for Self – Transformation*, Summit University Press, 2019

M.Doreal, MsD, PsyD, Kristen A. Vasques (illustrator), *The Emerald Tablets of Thoth the Atlantean*, Source Books Inc., 2006

Merriam Webster Dictionary *https://www.merriamwebster.com/dictionary/definition*

Mikao Usui, *History of Reiki, The Healing Touch by William Lee Rand*, Lotus Press, 1922

Oxford Dictionary
 https://www.oxfordlearnersdictionaries.com

Paramahansa Yogananda. *Autobiography of a Yogi, Crystal Clarity Publishers*, 2003

Pollack, Gerald. *The Fourth Phase of Water: Beyond Solid, Liquid and Vapor, Seattle, Wash.: Ebner & Sons*, 2013

Ronda Byrne, *The Secret, Atria Books*, 2006

Swami Sri Yukterwar, *The Holly Science, Martino Fine Books*, 2013

Three Initiates, *The Kybalion: A Study of the Hermitic Philosophy of Ancient Egypt and Greece*, 2011

www.ingramcontent.com/pod-product-compliance
Lightning Source LLC
Chambersburg PA
CBHW072128160426
43197CB00012B/2036